Praise for

# Kayak Cookery

" . . . Fun and practical tips for the weekend or expedition paddler . . . the most comprehensive food guide to the unique opportunity available to the kayak traveler."
    —Bob McPeters, associate buyer, Recreational
      Equipment Inc.

"Here is an end to trial and error in kayak cookery. Daniel's book more than fills the spot."
    —Beatrice Dowd, editor, *Sea Kayaking* magazine

"You could paddle a lifetime and still not use all the enticing, workable food ideas here."
    —June Fleming, author of *The Well-Fed Backpacker*

"Linda Daniel's book is a welcome addition to the sea rover's mess kit and will help turn any mundane beach buffet into a glorious outdoor banquet."
    —George Thomas, managing editor, *Canoe* magazine

" . . . A delight to read and to use . . . a wide knowledge and wealth of information to traditional camp cooking."
    —*Kayak Yak* newsletter

"Experience shows through Daniel's book. Her advice and her tips and recipes are all very relevant and useful. **Kayak Cookery** should have a place on your bookshelf."
    —John Ramwell, editor, *Advanced Sea Kayak Club*

"This new cookbook for the kayaker, canoeist, boater, and backpacker will help make freeze-dried menus obsolete."
    —Evergreen Equine Clinic

" . . . A nifty little paperback book."
    —Seattle *Post-Intelligencer*

# Kayak
# Cookery

## A Handbook of Provisions and Recipes

by Linda Daniel

First published spring 1988 by The Globe Pequot Press

Edited by Maureen Zimmerman
Designed by Judy Petry
Illustrated by Kris Wiltsie
Cover design and photography by Grant Tatum

Library of Congress Cataloging-in-Publication Data:

Daniel, Linda.
    Kayak cookery.
    Bibliography: p. 180
    Includes index.
    1. Outdoor cookery.   2. Kayak touring
I. Title
TX 823.D36    1986      641.5'78      86-20468
ISBN 0-89732-236-3

Manufactured in the United States of America

Distributed by The Globe Pequot Press

Second edition, second printing

Menasha Ridge Press
P.O. Box 43673
Birmingham, Alabama 35243
www.menasharidge.com

*In memory of my grandmother, Mimi, who loved to cook, especially when challenged to "make do." But when there was something new to see, her apron came off as quickly as she said, "Well, let's pick up and go."*

# Contents

# Acknowledgments

Every person on this list is going to say, "Who me?" That is the kind of people they are. For ideas, information, and expertise freely shared, and for the sustaining support of their interest in kayak cookery (the topic) and *Kayak Cookery* (the book), the author sincerely thanks:

— the hundreds of kayakers who have taken classes on the topic, and left the instructor with more than they took.

— Audrey Sutherland of Haleiwa, Hawaii, and Jill Thayer of Sitka, Alaska; they kindled the spark for the book.

— Thel Rollins of Seattle, Washington, for sharing recipes from the collection she is gathering from kayak-trip outfitters.

— Trudi Angell, David Arcese, Frieda Cron, Marcia Herrin, Judy and Lee Moyer, Diana Reetz-Stacy, Bill Ross, Tom Steinburn, Audrey Sutherland, Bill Turner, and Rana Fitzsimmons Wilcox–recipe contributors all.

— Jan Grant of King County and Olga Fusté of Pierce County, Washington State University Cooperative Extension agents, for consultation on food preservation.

— Carolyn Threadgill, Deborah Easter, Margaret Foster-Finan, Judy Petry, and Maureen Zimmerman. The author's manuscript is just the beginning; it takes a team of skilled professionals to make a book. This was an all-star team.

— Randel Washburne: paddling partner for many miles and many meals, fellow author/editor, and friend. He will eat anything once.

# Foreword

We came ashore at midafternoon on a day of steady rain at Glacier Bay. Halfway into a two-month trip, I knew what day it was in relation to tides and currents. But I had completely forgotten today was my birthday.

I pitched the big day-tent we use in wet weather and started the portable wood stove designed to use in it. Linda created some semblance of order from our jumble of gear and rummaged a bit in the bags.

Snack time! First appeared a carefully husbanded (and intact) package of water crackers with a tub of wine cheese spread. Then, to my amazement, came a little bottle of Black Russian cocktails—a particular favorite of mine—that had been chilling all day on the bottom of Linda's boat. She then produced folded-up birthday party hats and a dozen balloons. We took turns—one of us blowing up balloons and tying bunches to the tent, the other slicing fresh vegetables to stir-fry. A pot of rice steamed on the wood stove as shiitake mushrooms soaked nearby. We lingered over dinner. I had just blown out the candles on a cheesecake when we heard the tour boat approaching on its evening run up-bay. We had gotten to know the crew earlier, and I called them on the VHF radio: "There's wildlife ahead off your port bow." Park visitors dining aboard while watching miles of absolute wilderness roll by peered into the twilight drizzle to spy two well-fed, dry kayakers in party hats waving at them in front of a tent festooned with balloons.

Kayak touring with a home economist certainly added a new dimension to the experience, I thought with amusement. That had been foreshadowed on our first trip together in Southeast Alaska. We had come ashore to camp, and I was looking for tent space as Linda surveyed the beach for a kitchen site. "Look at all this counter space!" she hollered happily from within the pile of sand-scoured drift logs.

Kayak dining with Linda is a continuing adventure. I am forever surprised with edibles I had assumed were impractical to carry. But here they are, and no poor-relation simulations either: breakfast sausages identical to those back home (in fact they are the same, just dried and then rehydrated), fresh vegetables I discovered would last for eons, and combinations of plain supermarket things together with imagination, some dried vegies, and unusual spices and garnishes to produce a memorable dish rather than a pot of glop. And, for most of Linda's expedition recipes I owe the ultimate compliment: I would even eat the stuff at home.

Others agree. One rainy winter's night when four of us were paddling by a logging camp in search of a campsite, the caretaker invited us in to share his spacious, deserted quarters. Setting up in the gleaming stainless-steel kitchen designed to serve a small army of ravenous timber beasts, Linda cooked up one thing after another from our food bags, to the caretaker's amazed delight. Come morning departure time, he announced, "You guys can go, she stays!"

But Linda has mastered more than the art of gourmet cooking in the rough. Though kayaking provides the means and occasion for feasts of brought and foraged foods, there also are times when eating is just something to get done with and FAST is the primary ingredient of the recipe. Breakfasts must be speedy to catch an early current or just to get in distance before the afternoon winds. Then there are the evenings in trying conditions, when camp is little more than a beach bivouac in drizzle and dinner is one of the chores before bed. At those times I have most appreciated the premade dinners, complete with directions to encourage me through the few simple steps to edibility. On trips where miles per day are important and the wild country less hospitable, an array of such "mindless" dinners is an important element of my larder. I make them up for myself now, and rarely travel without a few tomato sauce "leathers" and vegetables I have dried.

Linda has shown me the art of making food complement the situation, from ways to get pleasantly and properly fed with the least fuss to turning simple ingredients into a celebration. I hope this book enriches your kayaking experiences as much as her innovations and common sense in beach cooking have mine.

Randel Washburne

# PART ONE

# About Kayak Cookery

# What is Special about Kayak Cookery ?

The surge of interest bringing thousands of newcomers to sea kayaking in recent years also has brought to the sport an incredible array of provisions, utensils, and ways of using them. This is not surprising, because most of those taking up kayak touring have come to it by way of other pursuits—backpacking, bicycle touring, cross-country skiing, whitewater kayaking, and river rafting, to name a few.

Each of those activities has its own well-developed tradition of cookery based on the experience of many participants. Introduce a neophyte to backpacking, and he or she is soon debating the merits of freeze-dried food. Take a newcomer on a week-long river trip, and that person comes back enamored of Dutch-oven cooking.

But until recently there has been little known and less said about the uniqueness of kayak cookery. Now, with camp cooks from many traditions taking what they know into a new setting, there is a burgeoning body of information about what does and does not work well. Borrowing and adapting from many sources while capitalizing on its unique legacy, sea kayaking is acquiring a culinary tradition of its own—with emphasis on the sea itself.

None of the other recreational pursuits has such a direct connection between its environment and its cookery. With sea kayaking comes seafood: crabbing, trolling for salmon while paddling, accepting a pair of giant clams from the geoduck divers whose operation you stop to watch. Likewise, the coastline offers a smorgasbord of intertidal life and foods that can be foraged along the shore.

A seagoing "flatwater" boat and the kind of touring it allows present a unique combination of challenges to the cook. Kayak cookery falls somewhere between the cuisines of backpacking and river rafting on the scale between ascetic and sumptuous. Backpackers eat within strict limitations imposed by the bulk and weight of what they carry. Rafters are unleashed by the possibilities introduced by ice chests, kitchen boxes, and heavyweight fare. Sea kayakers' limitations lie in between, and their inspiration derives from the bounty of sea and shore.

## Paddling a Big Cooler

Every sea kayak is, in effect, a floating cooler. Food placed in the bottom of the boat will be chilled to the temperature of the surrounding water. Even in the tropics, the water is certain to be cooler than the air in the heat of the day. In temperate regions, water in the fifty-degree range puts a nice chill on a bottle of wine.

To keep their cool, provisions in the bilge must be insulated from warmer air above. A layer of other provisions or gear will do the job. When packing food in a duffel or stuff sack, place the things that need cooling all along one side. Then place that side of the bag against the bottom of the boat.

The wine that comes in large (three-liter) cardboard boxes can be removed from its bulky box and laid in the boat in the plastic liner bag. But the prospect of puncture makes me feel insecure without a homemade packcloth bag into which the "wineskin" slips. Cut a hole in the cloth for the spigot, and when you get to camp, you can hang the whole thing from a tree. In warm weather, dip the bag in the ocean so evaporation cools the contents even more. (Remember the pictures of burlapped water bags hanging on the front of 1920s-vintage touring cars?) And when the wine is gone, do not throw the liner away. Use it for water or fill it with air to use as a cushion or give extra flotation to the boat.

I have seen kayaks that looked like produce barges, with carrots, cabbages, celery, onions, and oranges in the bilge. (I have also seen the look on the face of a paddler when he remembered the cabbage he had stuffed up into the bow five weeks ago. Its outer leaves looked pretty scruffy, but inside it was fine.)

"Free range" produce in the bilge is best kept to a minimum because the load can shift, unbalancing the boat. Also, loose pieces make the food a bother to retrieve at night. Left in the boat, it can attract insects and animals whose attention the boat is better off without. John Dowd, the author of *Sea Kayaking*, tells of an otter that took up residence in his cockpit and turned quite nasty at the suggestion he move on.

Hot sun beating down on the kayak's deck can help prepare dinner while you are paddling. Dry staples like beans and whole grains, not to mention home-dried or freeze-dried food, will cook much more quickly (minimizing the need to carry stove fuel) after a long, warm soak. Just put the food in fresh water in a poly bottle, screw on the cap and put the container just below the deck. (Salt water is not used for soaking or for reconstituting freeze-dried or home-dried foods because salt can inhibit absorption.)

A variation also well suited to sea kayaking is "haybox" cooking—wrapping insulation around a heated container of food. Bring a stew to the boiling point, then take it off the fire and insulate by burying it in a bag filled with Styrofoam pellets. The food will continue to cook for hours. (Boil ten minutes before serving.) Country folks for generations used that method, putting the pot into a box filled with hay. Nowadays, slow-cooking crockery pots do much the same thing. The abundant room in a kayak's hold can accommodate a soft-sided insulating rig. Try making it with the Styrofoam chips used in commercial packaging.

The same system works well for keeping things cold. On a spring trip in the San Juan Islands of Washington state, a frozen chicken still had not begun to thaw after thirty hours packed in this way.

Space beneath the deck also can provide a prime environment for growing fresh sprouts. Use a wide-mouth poly bottle, its mouth covered with cheesecloth, plastic (not metal) window screening, or a perforated cap sold to use with sprouts. Once a day, rinse the seeds and resulting sprouts with fresh water and then pour it off. Cap the container with its ventilated cover and stow just below the deck. Sprouts thrive in the warm, moist "greenhouse" atmosphere. They grow very slowly when cold, so keep them up off the bottom. The extra space in a kayak makes sprout growing much easier for both you and the sprouts than when using a plastic bag in a backpack. And on a lengthy trip, when much of the food you carry is dried, the fresh greens have tremendous appeal.

# Cooking with Salt Water

How many recipes begin with instructions to put fresh water into a pan and add salt? That does not make a lot of sense when you consider what is under the boat you are paddling. Cooking with salt water cuts down the amount of fresh water you need to carry—no small benefit when paddling in places like Baja California, where sources of fresh water are few and far between. It also minimizes the amount of salt to be carried (and clogged in the shaker by the moisture of salt air).

Sea water is far saltier than the salted water of standard cookery. It needs to be diluted with fresh water. Rule of thumb is to use a fifty/fifty mixture, half sea water and half fresh, when the cooking water will be discarded, not consumed. For example, the fifty/fifty combination is suggested for boiling spaghetti. When the water is going to be absorbed by the food, as when cooking rice, the standard proportion is one part sea water to two parts fresh. People who like less salt than typically used in mainstream American fare may wish to dilute sea water more than that.

But is sea water safe to use? In most cases, yes. The volume of water and action of the sea quickly dilute and dissipate contaminants. The best place to dip up cooking water is well offshore, where water moves freely, and away from settlements. (Within a busy marina, in any backwater, or downstream from a quaint rural village is NOT the place.)

Sea water is not unsafe for cooking just because it may be sparkling with phosphorescence or blooming with "red tide." Those phenomena, caused by plankton—microscopic sea life—will not harm humans consuming the water. However, shellfish from those waters COULD be poisonous. (See "Fishing and Foraging" for further information.)

# Gearing Up

A sea kayak is big enough to accommodate all sorts of unlikely cooking gear. On weekend trips I have packed along a hibachi (complete with charcoal and firestarter), an aluminum Dutch oven, a gallon thermos jug, and a small ice chest. That was before I discovered how simple life can be when you carry just a few complementary, multipurpose things. On month-long wilderness trips where the cargo capacity of two single kayaks was pushed to the limit, I learned not to take anything that could not do at least two jobs, and preferably three. We have winnowed things down to a basic set of cookware that goes on all trips and expands with the size of the group. (The larger the party, the more space for optional extra pieces and "toys" that are not essential, but can be fun.)

## The Basics

Traveling alone, I would carry the following:

**Backpacker's stove and fuel.** Ours is a Svea, which burns white gas. That means carrying at least one one-liter aluminum bottle of fuel. Stove accessories I consider essentials are a wind screen, a little tool for clearing a plugged gas jet (unless the stove is self-cleaning), and, of course, the key for adjusting the flame. I pack those two small items at the base of the stove.

**Cookset.** This consists of two nesting pots and a lid that will fit either one. The wind screen and stove fit inside for traveling, and I put the set in a plastic bag to protect my boat from soot.

Stainless steel cookware or aluminum? Stainless steel is impermeable to the cumulative damage done to aluminum by moisture in general and salt water in particular. To kayakers, heavier weight is not the drawback that encourages backpackers to choose the lighter aluminum cooksets. But stainless steel costs more—enough more to offset the shorter life of aluminum ware. We ended up replacing an old aluminum cookset with another one of the same kind. The deciding factor was that the aluminum pots are grooved to interlock securely into our stove's wind screen, making the whole thing less vulnerable to accidental spills. The most recent medical advice on the health hazard posed by aluminum cookware indicates you would have to be cooking in aluminum daily, year-round, and year after year, to get the degree of cumulative exposure that has been linked to Alzheimer's disease. Aluminum cookware for daily use at home may not be wise; aluminum cookware for camp cooking a month or two a year offers no significant risk.

**Pot-gripper.** You can make do with vise grips and, less successfully, with a couple of potholders. The pot-gripper is smaller and cheaper. Painting the handle a bright color helps to keep it from straying, as every pot-gripper I have known has tended to do.

**Skillet with nonstick coating and folding handle.** This type of skillet comes in several sizes; any will do. The greater capacity of larger ones comes in handy when making a stir-fry dinner for two or when grilling English muffins side by side. However, the pinpoint heat of a backpacker's stove does not evenly warm the entire surface of the larger pans.

**Small grill to use over a campfire.** My favorite is about two feet long, just big enough to accommodate both pots at the same time. These little grills usually are sold with backpacking gear. They are flat, with no moving parts, and simply lie across a couple of logs or rocks. We made a simple slipcase of packcloth to cover the fire-blackened grill for traveling.

**Dishwashing soap and scrubber.** No need to buy expensive saltwater soaps. Anything made with coconut oil will do. (Watch for bargain-priced coconut oil shampoo.) Some types of liquid detergent also do the job. We carry a small (about six-ounce) plastic flip-top bottle of dishwashing soap in the cookset along with a scrubber—a small dishwashing sponge encased in plastic mesh.

**Disposable lighter.** These inexpensive inventions of throwaway society have proven most reliable as fire starters in a marine environment. I carry two—one packed with the stove for everyday use and another in my emergency kit (where I also carry a waterproof case of paraffin-coated matches, a flint, and fire starter tablets). This paddler is not going to be stranded cold and wet!

**Swiss army knife.** Mine is ideal for the minimalist camp cook. It has two blades, a can opener, a screwdriver, and a corkscrew. The best place to keep it to make sure it will always be at hand is in your pants pocket, at the end of a lanyard clipped to a belt loop. (There are those who argue that this is not a good idea because if you forgot the knife was out and open, and suddenly jumped to your feet, the knife swinging at the end of its leash could injure you. I choose to take that risk, weighing it against the prospect of becoming separated from my knife.)

**One-cup drip coffee maker.** This plastic cone sits on top of a mug and holds just enough real coffee to brew a big cupful. No filters are needed.
   Some people say no coffee maker is needed; they simply use instant coffee. And now, to bridge the gap between those of us on opposite sides of the instant-versus-REAL-coffee issue, there have appeared on the market immersible bags of real coffee, similar to tea bags. The tradeoff is cost.

**Water jugs.** I carry a three-gallon collapsible plastic one as a reservoir, a two-quart poly bottle for camp use, and keep a one-quart bottle handy for drinking in the cockpit.

**Juice and liquor bottles, one of each.** Acid and alcohol interact with certain plastics and with aluminum (creating aluminum oxide in the latter case). So beverages containing acid or alcohol become contaminated when they are kept in containers made of those materials. Aluminum bottles with lacquer-coated insides are made for holding juice or liquor. They come in two colors, red and blue, so you can distinguish between the orange juice and the brandy without unscrewing the cap.

**Utensil roll.** Camping-goods stores sell variations on this theme of a roll-up container with pockets for cooking utensils and silverware. I like my homemade model best because it is made from a dish towel that dries what you insert. (See "How to Make a Utensil Roll," following, for details.) I pack the utensil roll just inside the food bag where it stays dry and easy to find. Rolled up in it is a plastic pancake turner, a big plastic spoon for stirring things in pots, a long-handled fork, a pair of chopsticks (handy for deep-frying), a table knife for spreading things like peanut butter, and an individual fork and spoon. (You really do not need the fork, insists the kayaker in whose company I once ate filet mignon with a soup spoon.)

**Aluminum foil.** A roll of foil is invaluable as a multipurpose aid to cooking, serving, and storing food. Heavyweight foil is not needed except for preparing certain foods, such as baked salmon or roast turkey. I like to carry a brand-new, small roll of standard-weight foil. You can leave the box and the inner core at home.

**Individual bowl.** Better than plates because they keep food warmer and can be used for any food (even filet mignon) are plastic bowls. The kind I like best are not really bowls, but the plastic tubs in which margarine is sold. Larger than bowls, they can better accommodate portions that match outdoor appetites. They also come complete with snap-on lids that let them double as containers for leftovers.

**Individual mug.** The unbreakable insulated kind is wonderful for keeping soup and hot beverages warm while you savor them on a chilly day.

## The Basics Plus One

When a second person joins a kayaker equipped with all of the above, the party of two will enjoy the added convenience of:

**One or two more pots.** I take a three-quart billy—an aluminum pot with a bail (a handle like that on a bucket). The big pot comes in handy for carrying and heating the amount of water two people use. The bail has been replaced several times. It comes in handy for all kinds of things, most recently standing in for a broken rudder shaft. The billy has a lid, making it usable as a Dutch oven. It was the largest of a set of nesting pots that came from Sears. Smallest of that set was a little one-quart pot with a lid and a pouring spout. Those two pots nicely complement the two in the cookset.

**Drip coffee pot.** Faster and more fuel-efficient than a percolater, a three-cup aluminum drip coffee pot from the variety store is ideal for campers who prefer ground coffee (and who would do violence to one another in attempting to share a one-cup coffee maker first thing in the morning).

**Additional water jug.**

**Additional individual water bottle (one quart), eating utensils, bowl, and mug.**

When two people travel in two single kayaks, it is wise to carry the cookset in one boat and the grill plus extra cookware (skillet, pots, coffee pot, foil) in the other. Then if the paddlers become separated, both will be equipped for cooking. Likewise, food can be prepared if equipment in one boat is lost in a capsize. As the size of a kayaking party increases, keep both cookware and food distributed among the boats.

## Three or More

Three or more campers are likely to need a second stove and cookset to accommodate the additional food they will prepare. Three can get by with equipment listed previously under "The Basics Plus One" if the third person brings personal utensils and a flat-bottomed wok to use in place of the skillet. A wok also works wonderfully for deep-frying with very little oil and can be used instead of a large pot. (Remove the wooden handle from the lid so that lid and wok nest together for compact carrying.)

For a party of four, double "The Basics" and substitute the wok for the two skillets.

---

### How to Make a Utensil Roll

Start with a sturdy dish towel or hand towel. Darker colors and patterned fabrics look less disreputable as they become soiled.

Place the towel face down, with one of the shorter ends toward you. Fold that end one third of the way up, as if the towel was a business letter being folded to go in a No. 10 envelope. Whipstitch the edges to secure the fold. You now have one big pocket.

Divide the big pocket in two with a vertical seam down the middle. Continue making vertical seams about two inches apart to create about eight deep and narrow pockets to hold individual utensils. Insert the utensils and fold the top edge of the towel down over them. Then, starting at the side, roll up the towel with utensils inside.

[*Continued on p. 23*]

---

Tack the middle of a two-foot-long shoelace or sturdy cord to the edge of the roll. Each end of the cord will be wrapped once or twice around the bundle and the ends tied to secure it.

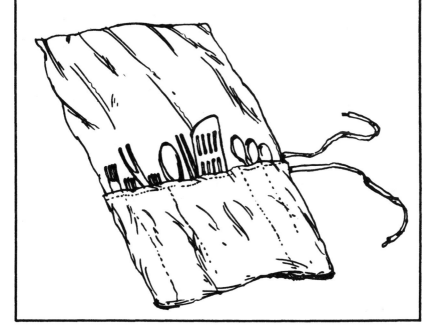

# Packing Down

Every time I pack food for a kayak trip I am amazed by the bulk of the packaging in which it comes. The key to carrying lots of food in very little space is leaving most of the store packaging at home. The key to making food easy to find and to fix in camp is repackaging it in a different way.

About a month in advance of leaving for a month-long trip, I commandeer a sofa and the coffee table in front of it. (Home decorating magazines speak of multipurpose rooms and furnishings, but somehow I do not think this is quite what they have in mind.) Among my blessings I count the second sofa at our house.

Returning from grocery-shopping forays, I sort the food onto the couch. Breakfast fixings go on the first cushion, lunch items on the middle one, and dinner makings on the third. General-purpose provisions, such as cooking oil and seasonings, go on the table top. As I keep bringing things home the stacks become mountainous. But, simultaneously, I am cutting them down a package or two at a time. Open the cardboard carton of six granola bars; throw the carton away; put the six bars (each individually wrapped in foil) into a zip locking bag. The bulk of the granola bars has been reduced by half.

Open the can of coffee. (The smell is a bonus.) Measure out the quantity needed for breakfast each day, then multiply it by the number of breakfasts you will cook. Pour the coffee into a plastic bag and seal with a twist-tie. (Zip locking bags are not the best choice for granular or powdered foods that have to be opened repeatedly. The food gets into the locking track and prevents a complete, secure seal.) The bulk of the coffee has been reduced dramatically (as has its weight, with the can left behind).

The process of packing is rewarding because your progress is so easy to see. And the work certainly is not hard if you do it a bit at a time. (Once I packed a month's provisions for two people in eight hours. Interesting as it was to know how much time such things take, the normally pleasant task turned into drudgery when I tried to do it all at a stretch. Never again!)

## Bags, Bottles, and Index Cards

Handy to have for packaging are plastic bags (the kind dispensed in the produce department) and twist-ties for closing them. At our house, twist-ties multiply like the ubiquitous wire coat hangers. Should you be concerned about having enough, save the big ones that come on bunches of asparagus and broccoli. Cut them into four-inch lengths.

Zip locking bags come in several sizes and at least two weights. Especially handy are one-quart and one-gallon sizes. I buy both the "storage bags" and the heavier "freezer bags." The lightweights are good for one-time use; the heavier ones stand up better to repeated openings.

Randel Washburne, author of *The Coastal Kayaker* and a frequent paddling partner of mine, often uses a Seal-A-Meal appliance, which packages food in airtight bags of whatever size you wish. Food odors do not escape and mingle as they do with other bags. The system also lends itself to boil-in-the-bag cooking. The drawback is that the packages cannot be resealed after opening. Bags for sealing come in both regular and heavy weights. With either one, you have to be careful not to seal the bag so tightly that sharp bits of food (such as pasta products and dried hash-brown potatoes) puncture the bag.

Also useful is a waterproof marking pen. Write on the plastic bag, labeling anything that needs it and adding instructions for preparation. "Powdered apple juice: mix one cup (a tiny measuring cup packed in with the powder) to one quart water," reads one of our bags.

Poly bottles, aluminum bottles, screw-top plastic jars, and other containers come into play. By the time you are done the piles will be much reduced in size. Also, it will be easy to see how much space the food will occupy and what size bags or other containers you will need to carry it.

For the ultimate in convenience food, go one step further and do some complete-meal packages. These are especially good on trips for which you do all of the food-buying and packing, but others will share the cooking chores. (Why in the world would you want to do something like that? Because others may be taking on other pretrip chores like arranging transportation, gathering and repairing equipment, or whatever they do best. Or because you have convinced them to pick up the tab for your transportation in return for organizing the common stores.)

In addition to assembling all the ingredients for the meal in one (or one set) of marked bags, include written instructions for preparing it. That way when somebody says, "What's for dinner?" you just say, "Here," and thrust the bag into those eager hands. There is everything the cook needs to know and you can continue your siesta undisturbed.

The ultimate in organization is to type up a four-by-six-inch recipe card for each dish. On the front goes the list of ingredients. Instructions for preparation go on the back. Then the whole thing gets a protective coating of waterproofing (paint-on variety or spray).

When planning a trip, browse through the collection of recipes, choosing those you would like to fix this time. Then it is off to the grocery stores, cards in hand. Who needs a shopping list? Everything already is listed there. Pack all ingredients for the dish into one plastic bag, then enclose the recipe with instructions for preparation on the back. Carry an extra zip locking bag in which to collect the cards after they are used in camp.

Now, I have never gotten a whole expedition that organized, nor do I think I would want to do so except when outfitting for a guided trip. But I certainly can appreciate the merits of the system. And on those occasions when I have used the cards, I have been impressed with the results.

## What Is in Which Boat?

The time that our party of four became separated and had to camp apart for a night I learned a lesson I will not forget. We had all of the food in our boats; they had all of the cooking equipment in theirs. (Yes, it is possible to fix a passable meal in a dishpan over a campfire and eat it with spoons carved from driftwood on the spot. Yes, they made it to a remote village that had a few groceries in the general store.) But the experience could have been pretty grim. And what if one of us had been stranded elsewhere or for a long time?

I always make sure that food and related paraphernalia are somewhat logically divided among all boats. What extra nuisance this entails before starting out the first time is more than offset by the insurance it affords everyone. It also makes it less likely that any piece of cooking equipment will be left behind, as the same person packs and carries the same things every time.

One system that works well is to parcel out the food according to meals. The makings of all breakfasts go into one bag, all lunch foods in another, and so on. Deal out one bag per boat for a party of four, two bags per boat for a twosome. More people will require more food, so you will need to double the number of dinner and general provisions bags.

A nice thing about this system is that for any meal, you need to open just two bags—the one for the meal and the general stores. It really minimizes rummaging.

## Packing Bags and Boat

The simplest way to pack food for kayaking is to put all food (packaged as described previously) into a stuff sack or duffel bag lined with a heavy-duty plastic garbage bag. Close the waterproof inner bag with one of those big twist-ties from a bunch of broccoli. Careful folding of the bag and wrapping with the wire will make it watertight. Then stuff in the ends and cinch up the protective outer bag. The inner bag is unlikely to puncture if you keep it inside the outer one. (I like to carry two inner bags side by side in a duffel bag, which gives easy access to the food inside and fits neatly ahead of my feet in the boat.)

Packing all food in this way keeps it watertight, protected in case of a capsize, a wave in the lap, or heavy rain on the beach. It also traps air, adding extra flotation to the boat. For flotation's sake you may wish to trap additional air in some of the bags.

Retailers of kayaking equipment sell air bags that hold gear and are contoured to fit in the bow and stern. These bags can be inflated to surround everything with air. Because food is heavy I prefer to carry most of mine closer to the center of the boat, but the bags can be used effectively. Also on the market are waterproof dry bags of many sizes and kinds. Protect them from puncture and abrasion, and they will serve well. Duct tape is good for making repairs in the field.

The way things are packed in a kayak affects its bouyancy, stability, and speed. None of that needs to be compromised in packing food to keep it in good shape.

General guidelines for boat-loading are to keep bow and stern lighter than the midsection, and to place the heaviest items on the bottom along the keel. In addition, make sure the boat sits squarely in the water, not listing to one side, and minimize the chance of gear shifting to throw off the balance when you are under way.

I usually keep the heavy food bag in the cockpit just forward of my feet. Within that bag, the heaviest items (such as canned foods) are on the bottom, lighter foods above them, and trapped air (as much as the bag will allow) on top. That air also insulates the food. If there is hot sun beating on the deck, I will put extra insulation on top of the food bag.

The second most weighty item is the water jug, which usually rides against the boat's bottom and centered just aft of my seat. Two poly bottles—one filled with drinking water, the other with juice—go low in the boat, one wedged on either side of the seat. The lunch bag also goes into the cockpit where it is easy to reach.

Early in a trip, when I am carrying both a heavy food bag and some fresh food I want to keep cool, the latter goes into a separate bag in the stern, against the bottom and just aft of the bulkhead separating cockpit and stern. Later, as provisions dwindle, all of the food ends up in the main food bag.

# The Kayaker's Kitchen

My paddling partner was still asleep as I crept from the tent to enjoy the world waking up in a pristine place. After a stroll on the beach I dipped water from a stream that ran near our campsite on its way to the sea. The smell of a fresh pot of coffee drew Randy from his sleeping bag. We each sipped a steaming cup, savored the brew—then spat it out.

"Mrs. Olson, my husband doesn't like my coffee," Randy wailed in parody of the classic TV commercial. "Well, Dear," he continued, this time in Mrs. Olson's motherly voice, "the secret to MY good coffee is that I make it with fresh water."

I had scooped water from the stream where it crossed the tideflat, running over sand still wet from the receding tide. Sea water and fresh water mingle both upstream and outward from the high-tide line, I learned that morning. For salt-free water, you need to go inland. How far depends on the terrain and the rate of flow of the stream. When you can no longer taste salt in the stream, you have gone far enough.

No, salinity does not eliminate the need for treating water to make it safe for drinking. And, because sea kayakers usually camp about as far downstream as you can get, they run a greater risk than do mountaineers of finding fresh water contaminated somewhere upstream by *Giardia lamblia*. It is an animal-borne microorganism that causes giardiasis, or "beaver fever," a particularly unpleasant and serious intestinal ailment. Current medical advice is to bring water to a rolling boil and maintain the boiling for a full minute to make it safe to drink. We usually keep two water jugs in camp, one filled with drinking water and the other with untreated water that can be boiled as we cook with it. Boiling a pot of water to refill drinking bottles and have enough to carry us through the next day is part of the after-dinner ritual. I feel best carrying a couple of gallons apiece in case we have to camp the next night at a place where there is no fresh water source.

Washing and rinsing dishes with salt water helps preserve the fresh water supply. A once-a-day washing with soap and hot water followed by a thorough rinse will prevent illness from food residue going bad or from lingering traces of soap. Remember to rinse coffee pot and cups in boiled FRESH water to avoid a Mrs. Olson scene.

Whether to use only biodegradable dishwashing suds is much more a matter of personal values on the ocean than in the hills, where it has a measurable impact. If you are tossing your dishwashing water into an outgoing tide where it will quickly be diluted in the vastness of the sea, your action will have infinitesimal consequences. You may be disturbing the balance of nature less than if you were walking on sensitive ground sprinkling biodegradable dishwater over a wide range. But the intertidal zone is an incredibly rich habitat, with literally hundreds of living organisms per cubic foot. Dumping directly on rocks or bottom exposed by the tide is inappropriate. Unlike ships flushing their tanks on the high seas, you would be delivering a concentrated dose of foreign substance to a very vulnerable habitat.

## Setting Up the Coastal Kitchen

One factor in choosing a campsite is a good kitchen site, protected from weather but with ample room to move around. In good weather, the beach is an appealing place—if you can keep sand from invading everything. The critical variable on the beach is the ever-changing tide. Consult the tide table before settling in. The swash marks of seaweed and driftwood that show the most recent high-tide lines are no guarantee the water will stop advancing at the same point tonight. This is especially important if you plan to call it a night before high tide, leaving a hot grill and other cooking gear at the kitchen site. Come back the next morning, and the place will look like the maid cleaned up after the party, sweeping the beach clean of footprints—and cookware as well.

Beach fires are not allowed in many areas because of the danger of fire spreading to the uplands. In state and provincial parks where there are fire rings or other designated campfire sites, the fire goes there, period. In other places where beach fires are allowed, there may be other restrictions. For example, in Glacier Bay the National Park Service allows fires only in the intertidal zone, where the tide will wash over the site.

By contrast, there are places—usually in rainy regions where fire danger is minimal—where the only rules governing beach fires are those of common sense. Build low on the beach, in collaboration with the tide, so the remains of your fire will be scattered to leave little trace and to minimize the chances of a lingering spark. Pick a place where there are no overhanging limbs from trees up on the bank. Do not build a fire against a drift log. It could smolder untended for days, possibly igniting other drift logs with or without rearranging by the tide. Drift logs make wonderful windbreaks. Many delightful evenings have been spent sheltered by them or sitting on top as a campfire glowed on the sand below. But a beach that has logs will have plenty of other materials with which to enclose the fire.

The best firewood a beach has to offer is the bleached and dried driftwood trapped behind logs at the highest high-tide line. Even if it has been rained upon, dried driftwood will dry and burn much more quickly than waterlogged wood recently deposited by the tide. (Knowing that, I once banked a fire with heavy, sodden timbers that had just been washed up. In the middle of the night, I awoke to see flames shooting thirty feet skyward from a huge bonfire down on the beach. My sodden logs had come from an old dock permeated with creosote.)

In building a fireplace, beware of rocks that are porous. When heated, the air inside them will expand. It can build up enough pressure to cause the rock to fracture or even to explode.

## Protecting the Food

Keep the food bags as cool as possible, ideally in deep shade and close at hand. Create your own shade, if necessary, cooling a hot spot before putting a food bag down on it. The bags will be cool on the bottom from contact with the bottom of the boat. Consider opening the inner bags to let any hot air escape from the top. Placing a wet towel over the bags will cool them by evaporation. And when hanging the bags during the day, pick a place where they will not be exposed to hot sun.

The coast has gulls, ravens, raccoons, bears, and rodents of varied stripe interested in the provisions you have brought. The safest place for food (and garbage, which smells just as interesting) is double-bagged in plastic and hanging in a tree. Packing food for kayaking usually results in double-bagging in the interests of waterproofing and flotation, so you will not need to bag another time to minimize the scent. Just hang the food bag(s) and relax at night or when you are away from camp during the day. Rule of thumb is to suspend it several feet off the ground and well away from the nearest trunk and limb. In bear country, increase the height off the ground and the distance from any trunk to fifteen feet and keep all food at least one hundred yards from the spot where you sleep. Hanging the food is a neat trick in upper Glacier Bay, where receding glaciers have left the terrain bare of trees. The Park Service there requires using bearproof food containers in all treeless places and loans the containers to campers heading up bay.

You may have heard the story about the camper who ate a chocolate bar just before sacking out. He awoke dreaming of his German shepherd, then discovered that the tongue slurping chocolate from his face belonged to a bear. Having no desire to share his experience, I am conscientious about washing my hands and face before retiring for the night in bear country. I do not take food into the tent where we sleep. Most of the time, I even remember to leave in the day camp the outer garment I wore while cooking and eating. I try to remember not to wipe my fingers on my pants.

But as custodian of the food in other regions, I may behave quite differently. After listening to the nighttime cacophony of San Juan Island's raccoons flinging every item of the cook kit, I once gathered all of the paraphernalia into my tent and slept undisturbed with a twenty-five-pound frozen salmon by my side. Even those brazen campground bandits will not (at this writing) invade an occupied and zipped-up tent.

Popular as paddlers' "food safes" in the San Juans are the large plastic jugs with big screw caps in which Greek olives are packed for export. Greek restaurants and delicatessens usually are happy to sell empty ones for a modest price. So far, nimble-fingered raccoons that can unlatch a Coleman cooler have not managed to open an olive jug with a tightly screwed-on cap, so the jugs may be appropriate alternatives to food-hanging in places known to be bear-free. However, my money is on the raccoons—and my food is either at my side or up a tree.

Never leave food in your kayak, either beached or anchored out. That boat is your transportation, and far too important to risk. Bears either angered or in quest of food have torn the fabric from aircraft and can peel a soft-skinned kayak like a banana. A mouse can gnaw through Hypalon as if it were so much packcloth. And even if the boat is not structurally damaged, a marauding animal can make an incredible mess with which to deal. Keep food in the boat only when you are in it too.

# Disposing of Trash

Some of the places sea kayakers visit do not have trash cans. There, the backpacker's "Pack it in, pack it out" ethic applies. But who wants to paddle a garbage scow? A practical solution is to burn all garbage and trash in the next fire. Almost anything made of aluminum will burn completely in a fire that is hot enough. Burn cans so there will be no lingering smell of food to attract animals. After the ashes have cooled, pick out cans and any other unburned material. Carry them in a plastic bag to which you add as the trip goes on. Dump it when you get into town.

Some kayakers deep-six beverage cans and other corrodable containers. I do not choose to do so, but if you do, make sure the containers are completely filled with water so they sink to the bottom. Beach combing in a remote spot where the drift logs have collected plastic bottles and other throwaway containers with half-lifes longer than human lifetimes will convince you never to discard anything that might eventually be cast up on shore. If in doubt, pack it out.

Leaving a campsite as you found it is always good advice, even when traveling in places where no other person is likely to set foot. I will admit to having given the remains of travel-weary rolls to ravens that were coveting them, but I would hate to paddle into a sheltered cove and find noodles floating in tide pools.

# Supermarket Shopping

Looking at the familiar supermarket through sea kayaker's eyes is like touring a place you have only glimpsed before. The shelves and cases are stocked with potential provisions: compact foods that are easy to fix in camp, keep a long time, and come out of the food bag still recognizable—even attractive. A reconnaissance trip to the biggest grocery store in town is a real eye-opener.

Pick a time when there are few shoppers, perhaps on a Saturday night. Take along a notebook to list, for later reference, the items with particular appeal. And plan to buy some intriguing things you have never tried before, to sample before taking them to sea. Such an outing can be great fun in the company of other sea kayakers, with each person (or pair of partners) taking an aisle and noting everything on it that has possibilities. When you have surveyed the whole store, buy the most irresistible refreshments to enjoy while comparing notes.

Many backpackers draw on this warehouse to supplement the outdoor stores' freeze-dried fare. The kayaker has an even wider range of choices because a kayak can carry more weight and bulk than a backpack. The kayaker's shopping cart could be mistaken for that of a sailor from the nearby marina, restocking his galley.

## Candy, Cookies, and Crackers

Candy bars go along on most trips to be eaten as part of lunches and for snacks. Kayaking burns up the calories that, for most people, put candy bars out of bounds for everyday eating. In addition to purchasing full-size bars, stockpile the smaller ones sold by the bagful around Halloween. Keep them in the freezer, taking out as many as you want for each trip. Big, foil-wrapped chocolate bars with special fillings are nice to savor along with after-dinner coffee or brandy. Hard fruit drops are pleasant accompaniments while paddling. The ones that are individually wrapped will not glue themselves together, as is the tendency after a few days on the water. I once came home with an interesting free-form sculpture of lemon drops.

Fig bars are the cookie of choice for outdoor recreation because of their forgiving ways when jammed into bag or pack. Topped with peanut butter, they provide a well-rounded energy-boosting snack. Other cookies that travel well are the soft oatmeal, molasses, and raisin-bar types stacked a dozen to a package. Ginger snaps are chosen not because they resist crushing, but because they taste so good crumbled into a bowl beneath hot applesauce or instant lemon pudding.

Sturdy crackers that come in a tight stack or armored by a crush-resistant package liner hold up best.

On trips where there is ample cargo space, you can accommodate corn chips that come in a cardboard cylinder about the size of an oatmeal box. Also sturdy enough to survive some traveling are the tortilla chips sold in large, reclosable plastic bags.

## Baking Supplies

Cheesecake may sound imposing, but it is not hard to make in camp. Just buy a mix for a cheesecake that does not need baking, add a candle, and you are ready to celebrate a birthday. (See "Recipes" for details.)

Gingerbread mix turns into a nondescript-looking but tasty dessert poured just as it comes from the box into applesauce, then simmered to the texture of pudding. A more refined concoction is gingerbread dumplings. Mix the gingerbread batter and drop it a spoonful at a time into a hot potful of applesauce. For best results, use just enough water to make the gingerbread mix into a thick but pourable dough. Hold a blob of it on the spoon until it cooks enough to hold its shape, then set it free to float on top of the applesauce and finish cooking while you launch additional dumplings.

Almost any brownie, cake, or muffin mix can be cooked as pan bread. The secret is to do it over low heat and turn frequently. Consider Snack'n Cakes and Jiffy muffin mixes, all of the right size to serve four. Jiffy brand corn muffin mix is especially versatile. I use it for corn pancakes (to serve with hot, real maple syrup) and to drop dumpling-style atop a simmering pot of chili. Corn muffin batter also can be deep-fried as hush puppies.

Any yellow cake mix lends itself to being steamed as dumplings or cobbler on top of a hot pot of fruit (with plenty of juice). Line the pot with foil to make light duty of an otherwise gummy cleanup job.

All-purpose baking mixes (which can be duplicated from scratch at home) are handy because they can produce biscuits, dumplings, pancakes, and various other quick breads through simple variations on the mixing theme. Read the package for details, and see Missouri Mix under "Recipes."

In choosing a pancake mix, look for a brand that needs nothing but water to mix. And ask yourself if you really will need it if you also are taking corn muffin mix and all-purpose baking mix. Syrup is best carried in a screw-top plastic bottle (which can be uncapped and set upright in a pot of hot water to warm while the pancakes are frying). Small packets of syrup given out at fast-food restaurants have an unfortunate tendency to rupture in the food bag.

For fast and simple camp cooking, open the boxed mixes at home and add powdered egg and milk in appropriate quantities. Seal each mix in a zip locking bag and use a waterproof felt-tip pen to write on the bag what it contains and how much water to add. In camp, just open the bag, pour in the water, reclose the bag and knead until the batter is mixed.

The easiest way to put real butter flavor into foods prepared far away from the dairy case is with Butter Buds, a granulated product sold in premeasured packets. Look for it among baking products or on the grocery shelves near canned and powdered milk.

## Fruits and Juices

Many dried fruits (apples, apricots, prunes, figs, and assorted fruits) are sold in plastic bags, ready to carry. Close the top with a twist-tie after opening. You probably will have to repackage dates, raisins, and currants to eliminate their cardboard boxes. An increasing number of grocery stores are selling dried fruits in bulk bins, from which you can select exactly the right amount for your trip and plastic-bag it on the spot.

Fruit leathers are sold both individually and by the box, often in two different parts of the store. Be sure to compare ingredients as well as price, as some contain much less fruit than the pictures on the packaging suggest.

Careful label-reading also is called for when confronting powdered fruit drinks and juice crystals. Some are all fruit, some are sugar with fruit flavoring, and some are in between those extremes and may be fortified with vitamin C. Weigh them (literally) against the fruit juices and fruit drinks in little foil pouches and foil-lined boxes with straws attached. Carrying a week's worth of the latter is a lot of weight, but it may be a good choice if you are going to Washington state's San Juan Islands, where there is no fresh water in most campgrounds in summer months. And, as in the case of the powdered lightweights, read labels to find out if you are getting 100 percent fruit juice or a fruit-flavored drink that is only part juice.

One of the best fruit buys for kayakers is the juice-filled plastic "homestead lemon" (a kitchen staple in wilderness cabins and isolated homes). Appropriately (and recognizably) packaged for the paddler's pantry, it affords juice to squirt on fresh-caught fish, to spark a sweet fruit cobbler, to add a fresh taste to the water in a drinking bottle, or to make lemonade (two tablespoons lemon juice plus one teaspoon honey to each cup water).

Often available in grocery stores is jug wine in foil-lined cardboard boxes, complete with spigots, an economical, ready-packed choice. It may not be what you would serve at a dinner party in town, but it adds an elegant touch to kayak-camp cuisine.

## Coffee, Tea, Cocoa, and Milk Products

Those who prefer ground coffee to its instant counterpart might wish to try the high-yield types. For example, a fraction more than two pounds of one brand of high-yield "flaked" coffee brews up as many cups as three pounds of the same brand's conventional grind.

The aroma of coffee permeates zip locking bags, which can produce a mocha surprise when coffee is packed next to chocolate. Less pleasing is the result when coffee rides next to Cheddar cheese. Double-bagging does what most people consider an adequate job of keeping the coffee aroma where it belongs. Others carry their reserves of coffee in aroma-proof Seal-a-Meal packets.

The world of instant coffee is not to be written off. On the grocery shelves, coffee is a many-flavored thing with international pretensions. There even is a quite passable instant espresso.

When it comes to tea, consider the instant blends such as Constant Comment (flavored with orange and spice) and the iced tea mixes (usually flavored with lemon and sweetened). They are equally good hot or cold. In choosing noninstant tea, look for tea bags sealed in individual foil packets.

As for hot chocolate, choose single-serving packets of a brand that contains milk or add your own dry milk powder to a batch of the other kind. (There are few things as pleasant in camp as a nightcap of hot chocolate to which has been added a little brandy, instant coffee, or peppermint extract.)

And while on the subject of dry milk powder, the instant nonfat kind is easy to mix successfully in camp. Choose Milkman brand "with the kiss of cream" for the taste closest to whole milk. (Dried whole milk is widely sold in Mexico, but not in the United States.) As an alternative, add a can of evaporated milk to a quart of nonfat milk made from powder. For real-milk diehards, there are cartons of super-pasteurized milk that need no refrigeration. Look for them on the grocery shelves with powdered and canned milk.

## Breakfast Foods

Hot cereals cook at three speeds: instant (add boiling water and stir), quick-cooking (stir into boiling water, cook for up to five minutes), and regular (cook twenty minutes or so). Instant cereals, many of which come in single-serving packets, are dear to the hearts of those who like to hit the water early with a minimum of food-fixing and cleanup. The quick-cooking cereals usually have better flavor and texture. The regular ones generally have the greatest nutritional value, and can be presoaked, precooked, or prepared overnight to speed things the next day. (See "Recipes" for details.)

A stick-to-your-ribs breakfast rich in carbohydrates and protein is a bowl of cream of wheat with about three tablespoonsful of peanut butter stirred in. The taste is not a difficult one to acquire.

For cold-breakfast eaters, the grocery shelves are a cornucopia of granolas, granola bars, and breakfast bars. My stepchildren grew to adulthood with no untoward effects from campground breakfasting on cold Pop Tarts.

## Prepared Dinners

In *The White-Water River Book*, Ron Watters tells of river-running on Maypo cereal and Lipton Dinners until he could no longer stomach either one. That says something good about both products, so appropriate as outdoor fare that they invited overdosing. It also suggests that diversification is a good thing in the face of the easy solutions the packaged dinners present. The old Lipton Dinners in funny-shaped boxes of which Watters wrote are no longer. Kayakers join backpackers in mourning their passing. But meet the new Lipton products along with Rice A Roni, Hamburger Helper, and shelfmates! Read boxes, pick the ones that lend themselves to camp preparation, and you can be on your way.

Another favorite in this section is long grain and wild rice, which comes in both regular and quick-cooking varieties. Either is superb with fresh-caught fish (or the backup from the tuna can). Often overlooked are the stove-top stuffing mixes, easy to fix over campstove or fire. Combine one in the same pot with turkey gravy from a packaged mix, freeze-dried diced chicken, and green peas; serve with cranberry sauce; give thanks.

Betty Crocker hash brown potatoes are featherweight to pack, but rehydrate into a crispy mountain of fresh-tasting fries. Try them with deep-fried cod as fish and chips. Other dry potato mixes, such as scalloped and au gratin, can be the foundation of tasty one-pot meals. Just stir your choice of vegetables and meat into the sauce.

Canned chili tastes wonderful outdoors. Carry the can or dry the contents at home for a lightweight package. The same goes for canned hash, both corned beef and roast beef varieties. One canful makes a hearty breakfast that will keep two kayakers going for half a day.

Lightweight contenders that can handle heavy duty include all of the ramen-type noodle dinners (add meat and vegetables to make a meal) and dry tortellini, little rings of pasta filled with cheese. And in the pasta section, look for rotini, the corkscrew-shaped noodles that hold a lot of sauce and yet are easy to handle sans colander and serving tools.

Inspired by the combinations of ingredients listed on packaged dinners, consider custom-mixing your own with a base of pasta, rice, or dry beans. To make that easy, survey what is in the sauce and soup aisle.

## Sauces and Soups

Little foil packets of mixes hold the secret to sauces like hollandaise, cheese, and sour cream. Then there are gravy mixes and soup packets (such as cream of leek and cream of asparagus) that make sauce as well as soup. Pick a sauce (let's start with cream of mushroom), add a meat (canned chicken), and a vegetable (fresh broccoli). Serve it over brown rice. Next time, combine cheese sauce with bits of salami and fresh onion, and spoon it over buttery noodles. How about cream of asparagus soup with fresh asparagus added along with fresh crab and a splash of sherry? Serve it over a baked potato fresh from the coals.

Among the soups, there are individual servings of dried ingredients that burst into soup in your mug when hot water is added. These soups and foil packets of bouillon are wonderful to have handy when you need something hot and nourishing and EASY to fix. For the more leisurely meal, choose a mix that gives you the fragrant, seasoned stock for a fresh stew. Choose spicy "crab and shrimp boil" or classic bouillabaisse.

## Canned Meats and Fish

Hygrade's West Virginia Brand Crumbled Bacon gives you real bacon bits in a can that needs no refrigeration. The snap-on plastic cap will protect the leftover portion for the following day. Think omelets and sour cream-sauced potatoes and hearty split pea soup.

My favorite of the canned fish is kipper snacks. We like them for breakfast, heated in the can and served between two toasted halves of English muffin. Canned tuna and chicken are reliable standbys for one-pot meals on the night you planned to have fresh fish, but the fish did not come.

## Deli Case

Look at what is displayed outside the refrigerated case: pepperoni, hard salami, jerky, beef sticks, individual summer sausages. These will keep for months, even in hot weather. (Note: Strong-smelling salami is attractive to bears, more than one kayaker in Alaska has found.)

Smoked, vacuum-packed meats will keep several days on the cool bottom of the boat. We took a whole smoked turkey to Thanksgiving dinner in camp.

Dressed for kayaking are the cheeses wrapped in foil or encased in wax. Individual rounds of Bonbel are perfect for lunch bags. So are the cheese spreads in plastic tubs, vacuum-packed mozzarella string cheese, canned Camembert and Brie. Any hard cheese such as Cheddar or Swiss will keep indefinitely if you cut it into chunks of a size to last for a couple of days, wrap them in cheesecloth, and dip in paraffin. Parmesan cheese comes in two forms well suited to kayaking: the cylindrical shaker boxes of dry cheese (which will need to travel in a plastic bag to keep moisture out) or a chunk of fresh Parmesan wrapped in cheesecloth and then in plastic. Grate it off meal by meal.

## Bakery

English muffins are almost indestructible. They have traveled with us for more than two weeks. Plain and sourdough flavors are the most versatile for everything from peanut butter sandwiches to garlic toast, but the raisin muffins offer a pleasant change of pace. Bagels, which also come in a range of flavors, are stalwarts of the kayaker's stores. Other sturdy breads include party rye and unsliced loaves of heavy textured, dense sourdough, rye, and some wheats.

## Miscellaneous

Peppy's Fish Batter, a dry mix to which you add nothing but water, is wonderful for deep-frying chunks of fresh rockfish. For all-purpose use, carry margarine (the kind sold in plastic tubs), which lasts indefinitely. For a taste approximating real butter flavor, try Butter Buds granules.

And finally, I rarely leave home without instant pudding. Served warm or cold, it is a pleasant way to end the day (and get in a serving of milk that paddlers might otherwise miss). Splash a little rum over butterscotch pudding, brandy over chocolate, and anything over vanilla. Use up leftover rice in rice pudding: just mix together vanilla pudding, a teaspoon of cinnamon, and cooked rice in any amount up to a cup.

# From the Natural Foods Store

You certainly need not be a natural foods enthusiast to be enthusiastic about a well-stocked "health food" store. Many products sold in these stores are naturals for kayaking. Among them are foods sold in bulk so you can buy precisely the amount you need for a recipe or to fill a container for traveling. For example, campers who carry the multi-compartment containers of spices sold at outdoor recreation stores (or 35-millimeter film canisters of herbs and spices) can refill them as needed. You just take the containers to the store, weigh them when you get there, fill them, weigh again, and pay for the difference.

## From Barrels and Bins

Pasta of all shapes and in a rainbow of colors can be purchased by the pound. Figure that you will need about six ounces of dry pasta to feed each hungry kayaker. Although green pasta, made with spinach, is common these days in supermarkets, you are not likely to find the complete spectrum there. Try whole wheat lasagne or elbow macaroni in bright yellow, pink, or beige (made with corn, dried tomato powder, and whole wheat, respectively). The different flavors, colors, and textures add variety and interest to camp meals.

Dry beans, peas, and lentils also come in more varieties than can be found sealed in plastic in grocery stores. They usually are less expensive bought in bulk. Scoop the amount you want into a plastic bag at the store, close it with a twist-tie, and your legumes are ready to travel. You can bag them in the exact amounts specified in recipes, so there is no measuring to do at home (and no half-filled bag to lurk in your cupboard, no cardboard box to discard).

Rice also is sold in bulk. Choose white, brown, or wild rice (really not a rice at all, but a grass). Information on the bulk bins will tell you how long it takes to cook each kind and how each one differs in flavor, texture, and nutritional value. Take along some short-grain white rice that cooks up just like the wonderful sticky stuff served in Japanese restaurants; serve it with stir-fried vegetables in camp. And instead of a more costly box of commercially packed long grain and wild rice, mix two ingredients yourself—one part wild rice to three parts brown rice.

Nuts and seeds of many kinds add variety to lunches and snacks. Salted corn nuts, pumpkin seeds, soy nuts, and sunflower seeds coated with tamari are among the more unusual ones. Fresh, raw cashews are as different from the roasted, salted ones as are fresh-picked garden peas from those in a can. Try roasted pistachios or soy nuts. You could have something different every day of your trip.

Granola of several kinds, each containing a different blend of grains and nuts, is sold in bulk. So is trail mix or gorp (which stands for "good old raisins and peanuts," but usually contains the traveler's favorite dried fruits, nuts, and carob or chocolate). For those who want to custom-mix their own granola or gorp, a world of possible ingredients is right at hand.

Popcorn also is sold in bulk, and almost always much less expensively than in the grocery store packages you throw away. Look elsewhere in the store for intriguing popcorn seasonings to vary the flavor of this nutritious snack that is compact and long-lasting, ideal for a kayak trip.

Hearty multigrain cereals are among other bargains, as are seeds of several kinds for growing fresh sprouts. But my favorites are the kegs of honey with spigots from which to refill my squeeze bottle and the machine that grinds fresh peanuts into peanut butter and oozes it right into my screw-top jar.

## Dried Products

In addition to the herbs and spices mentioned at the beginning of this chapter, expect to find all sorts of dried fruits and vegetables. Light-weight and long-lasting without refrigeration, these beg to go kayaking. Among the fruits are apple chips (fresh apple rings dried crispy for snacking), nectarines, and cherries. All of these are drier, and conse-quently lighter, than the packages of dried fruits sold in grocery stores. Look for little nuggets made of dates and dusted with dry date powder so they do not stick to your fingers or to everything else in the trail mix or granola.

Dried vegetables include whole tomatoes, wonderful to munch straight from the sack and ideal for rehydrating in one-pot meals. I espe-cially like them mixed into macaroni and cheese. You also can buy dried flakes of tomatoes, green peppers, spinach, onions, and others. They re-hydrate instantly. Stir them into a ramen-type noodle dinner, use them to fill an omelet, or toss them by the handful into one-pot meals.

Also handy for adding meat flavor and texture to casserole-type dishes is textured vegetable protein, commonly called TVP. It is a dried soybean product that usually comes flavored and crumbled to resemble ground beef. It needs no refrigeration, and reconstitutes instantly. Add it to spaghetti sauce or use it in enchiladas or tamale pie. A T-bone steak it is not, but it does a good job of standing in for meat in highly spiced dishes like those just suggested. (Do not stir the pot too much after add-ing, or you will end up with UN-textured vegetable protein.)

Dried egg powder and dried milk powder both can be bought in bulk at the health food store for a fraction of the cost of their packaged counterparts sold among camping supplies. By contrast, you may find it more costly to buy fruit leathers and granola bars. Read the label and you will see why. These leathers are likely to be 100 percent fruit instead of sugar, water, and fruit flavoring. (Ingredients are listed in order of their proportions in the finished product. The first ingredient is the one used in largest quantity.) In comparing granola bars, consider that whole grains have greater nutritional value than do refined ones.

While in the vicinity of snacks, look for energy bars, pemmican, and other super-concentrated foods. They are meals in themselves, handy to keep in the cockpit to sustain energy while paddling, and serve well as emergency rations.

## Crackers and Bread

Sturdy crackers that stand up to stuffing into bags and boats are easy to find at the natural foods store. Whole-grain products are by their nature more sturdy than light in texture. A cracker born to go to sea is Pilot Bread, carried aboard ships of all sizes, including kayaks. Big wheels of Swedish rye crispbread are the forerunners of Rye Krisp. Solid crackers of other kinds include stone-ground sesame and high-fiber rye with wheat bran.

Fig bars travel very well, and they come in several variations on the basic theme. Those made of whole wheat stay moist longer and crumble less.

Over in the "fresh today" bread section, look for pita (pocket) bread, wheat hamburger rolls, onion buns, and the like for making sandwiches early in your trip. Sliced sandwich bread just does not hold up. However, a fresh-baked loaf that has not been sliced would be appropriate, especially if it has a heavy, whole-grain texture.

## Other Discoveries

Brand names you do not see in supermarkets can be found in natural foods stores. Many of these manufacturers specialize in products made without preservatives or with "all natural" ingredients. They can add interesting variety to camp meals. Look at dried soup mixes, where you might find something as unusual as Spanish gazpacho. Packets of sauces and gravy mixes can be the starting point for many an easy-to-improvise one-pot meal.

You will find interesting and nutritious hot cereals. No, they are not all time-consuming to prepare. The quick-cooking and instant varieties are there, too. Consider Kashi, a breakfast pilaf that is good either hot or cold, and excellent topped with fresh yogurt. And among cold cereals, there is müesli, a Swiss-style granola that may include maple sugar or fruit and nuts.

Almost all natural foods stores carry packaged, dry mixes for making hummus and tabbouleh by just adding water. These are perfect to take kayaking. Hummus is a tasty Middle Eastern appetizer made of mashed garbanzos with seasonings. Stir up a batch in camp and serve it as dip for fresh vegetables—carrot sticks, celery, sliced turnip, green pepper strips, broccoli and cauliflower florets Tabbouleh also comes from the Middle East. It is a hearty salad based on cracked wheat. Add chopped fresh tomato and cucumber when circumstances permit. Otherwise, toss in some dried tomato flakes. Elsewhere in the store you will find the ingredients for making both of these dishes from scratch, but the mixes, made for the American market, are ideal for trip provisioning.

# Foreign Groceries and Specialty Foods

Whether they come from food stores serving an ethnic community or a supermarket's "foreign foods" shelves, certain foods from other countries are ideal for kayaking. Some may inspire campsite preparation of an authentic dish, perhaps a stir-fry with Japanese shiitake mushrooms in the wok. Others may simplify camp preparation of mainstream American dishes, as does quick-cooking Mexican masa used in place of cornmeal. And some of these items are not at all "foreign" in the sense of being unfamiliar; it is just that they derive directly from the cuisine of another land.

## Mexican

Tortillas, both those made of corn and the larger ones made of flour, are forgiving of tight packing and last longer than most breads. They can enclose lunch meats and cheese, even peanut butter, as well as more authentic fillings such as refried beans. The beans come canned, ready to heat, and can be easily dried at home to save space and weight. Also sold in Mexican markets and in natural foods stores is boxed "frijoles mix," dehydrated refried beans.

Masa is cornmeal processed to use in making tortillas; just add water and fry. You can do it in camp after your last store-bought tortilla is gone. Using masa in place of cornmeal in dishes like tamale pie saves precious campstove fuel because of the much-shortened cooking time.

Packets of dry chili mix give you all the fixings for a flavorful one-pot dinner; just add water and beans. Long-distance paddlers probably will want to use economical and long-lasting dry pinto, red, or kidney beans.

Mild, green chili peppers add personality to bland refried beans, burritos, and egg-and-cheese dishes. Most stores carry them in cans. They are quick and easy to home-dry straight from the can.

Enchilada sauce comes canned (mild or hot) and in packets of dry ingredients. The milder sauce can be used undiluted or slightly thinned with water; the hotter sauce usually calls for dilution with tomato sauce or canned tomato soup. For maximum compactness, choose the dry sauce mix and any dry tomato soup mix.

Those who visit Mexico may come home enamored of Ibarra sweet chocolate, seasoned with almonds and cinnamon. Shaved into a cup of hot milk (which can be made from dry milk and hot water), it makes a memorable cup of hot chocolate. The chunks of seasoned chocolate also are great for nibbling to boost energy and take in some of the extra fats needed by those consuming large quantities of dried provisions.

# Asian

Tempura batter mix offers a delightful alternative to ordinary deep-frying of fish. Use it with seafood that you catch and round out the meal with tempura-fried wedges of carrot, onion rings, and whole green beans.

Packets of blended seasonings put sweet-and-sour dishes, authentically flavored stir-fries, and teriyaki at a paddler's fingertips. One big fish can come to dinner in so many different guises that there is no risk of boredom. Also, use the teriyaki sauce as a marinade for home-dried jerky.

To season a stir-fry from scratch, which might be the way to go if you plan to use this cooking method often, consider preseasoned wok oil (already flavored with garlic and ginger) or stock up on toasted sesame oil and fresh ginger. Canned vegetables that would make a magnificent meal for a weekend kayaking party include water chestnuts, lotus root, and bamboo shoots. (Do not forget the fresh bok choy.) Consider buying soy sauce in individual packets.

Dried garlic slices, shallots, and mushrooms are all-purpose ingredients. In a class by themselves are the distinctively flavored Japanese shiitake mushrooms, which transform a run-of-the-mill stir-fry or make something special of a ramen-type noodle dinner. These come in many combinations of flavored broths and different noodles. And the exotic pastas are all there to buy separately and use in noodle innovations of your own. Try bean threads (transparent noodles), rice noodles, wheat noodles, buckwheat noodles, rice vermicelli, and other rice noodles.

Miso soup is a nourishing, delicious base for a noodle supper. (We carry a few of the very small, individual foil packets of instant miso soup in our emergency survival kits.)

For a pleasant change of pace try Chinese-style jerky of beef or pork, sold in many flavors. Vary the daily munchies with some bright green Japanese dry, fried peas. And for amusement as well as snacking, deep-fry some shrimp-flavored chips—multicolored, almost weightless bits that balloon in hot oil and are delicious eaten hot, on the spot.

As a change from your everyday rice, pack some of the Chinese glutinous kind to go with your most authentic stir-fry dishes, and some Basmati rice to serve with curries. Look for S&B brand curry sauce mix. Inside a cardboard box is a bar of semidry substance that you crumble into a pan with water to make a rich, full-flavored curry sauce. Read the fine print on the box: "medium hot" pleases most Western palates, "hot" will probably bring tears to your eyes.

## European

Rich chutneys of several flavors (to contrast with that fiery curry) are among imports from the British Isles. So is rich Scottish shortbread, one of the sturdiest cookies in existence.

From Switzerland comes müesli, the forerunner of granola. It is good eaten dry or with milk, but exceptional stirred into plain yogurt and allowed to stand overnight or at least a few minutes before eating. Also from the Swiss come Tisa brand beverage cubes for hot drinks flavored with rose hips, fruit, chamomile, and peppermint.

Continental specialties ideal for kayak trips include hard breads made in loaves about four inches square. The most common varieties are cocktail rye, limpa rye, and pumpernickel. They travel exceptionally well. So do the canned breads (usually rye and pumpernickel) and "common crackers," the kind that used to be stored for months in open barrels in the general store.

The French have thoughtfully packed sandwich cookies in rolls to prevent pulverizing. And a can of French pâté makes an elegant appetizer for special occasions. So does canned herring in tomato, paprika, or curry sauce.

Going beyond the range of dried soups and sauces widely sold in the United States are their European counterparts. Try hunter sauce, pesto for pasta, and the excellent hearty soups that come dehydrated in sealed packets. Norway exports magnificent dry mixes for seafood chowder and crab, lobster, or shrimp bisque. (For pure decadence, try any bisque laced with your own sherry.) For everyday use, consider fish-flavor bouillon, not usually sold in this country. And a real boon to kayak cookery is concentrated garlic paste, tomato paste, and onion paste in tubes.

The Europeans do imaginative things with puddings, and package the makings in highly concentrated powders. From Germany comes a classic. Dr. Oetker Paradies Creme instant pudding powder in flavors that include creme-caramel, raspberry, chocolate, and lemon. Under the French label Ancel Entrements you will find flan (a rich egg custard), coffee, vanilla, and chocolate puddings. All come in packets that make enough to serve four.

# Canadian

Food products sold in Canada closely resemble those of the United States, but some of the packaging makes the Canadian products much handier for kayakers' use.

For example, the Canadians first introduced "teabag coffee," real coffee in individual, immersible bags just like tea. It comes in both regular and decaffeinated.

On the grocery shelves with canned vegetables you will find freeze-dried vegetables as well. The packet of freeze-dried peas I bought in a Canadian supermarket cost less than one-fourth as much as the same quantity from an outdoor recreation store in the United States. Quality, so far as I could tell, was identical.

Also widely sold in Canada are unique maple sugar products. Canada leads the world in production of maple sugar, and in recent years has been selling it in some attractive new forms. Buy them in gift shops that cater to tourists, and you will pay a premium price. For substantial savings, look for them in larger grocery stores. Absolutely indispensable nowadays to me are pure maple sugar crystals. Sprinkle them on hot cereal or warm, buttered English muffins. Or, best of all, mix them with a little water and you have real maple syrup.

Canadian grocery stores also sell English muffins and crumpets at everyday prices, below what we pay in the United States.

# Cheese and Specialty Shops

A visit to a cheese shop can provide kayakers with not only out-of-the-ordinary cheese for short trips, but longer-lasting provisions than those commonly sold in grocery stores. For example, expect to find many more cheeses encased in wax. Also look for dry cheese as hard as the chunks of Parmesan familiar to most of us. They are the cheeses with the longest unrefrigerated shelf life. Among them are hard versions of Cheddar, Swiss, jack, and less familiar cheeses such as asiago.

To carry hard cheeses in a hot climate, simply wrap in several layers of cheesecloth and allow the package to "breathe" as often as traveling permits. To protect any cheese, give it a wax jacket before you leave. Cut chunks of a size that will last you a few days, wrap in a couple of layers of cheesecloth, and dip in melted paraffin to seal. Cheese carried unprotected by wax (or by a sealed plastic or foil wrap) quickly deteriorates as it is opened and closed from day to day. Several smaller pieces travel much better than one large chunk.

Specialty shops that sell cheeses often carry related items, such as crackers, that are worth checking out. Also look for special mustards and tinned appetizers such as smoked salmon, smoked oysters, and sardines. And occasionally you will encounter dried chanterelles, wild mushrooms much prized by gourmets.

# Fresh Starts

Savoring fresh food is one of the pleasures of kayak touring, whether the trip is for a day, a weekend, a week, or more. Almost anything can be taken on a short outing, and a surprising number of fresh foods will last longer than that. In much the same way as kayaking puts paddlers in tune with the natural rhythms of weather and tide, working within the limits of fresh foods' staying power is a refreshing challenge to many who are used to simply opening the refrigerator door. The trick is to seize the chance to enjoy fresh foods at their peak and interplay them with "anytime" fare as the fresh supplies dwindle, falling back on dried and canned provisions until you reach a new port and restock with whatever happens to be there. Just as in fishing and foraging, there is pleasure and surprise in reprovisioning along the way.

Fresh means perishable. How long will fresh food last on a kayak trip? That depends not just on what it is, but also on how it is stored. Start with the freshest of the fresh, looking at the "pull dates" that many states require on dairy products and baked goods. Pick fruits and vegetables that are perfect, not bruised or past their prime. Choose some fruits that will ripen just about the time you have finished those that started off ripe. Do your fresh-food shopping just before departure, and handle the food as little as possible to extend its life.

Keeping food cold slows the deterioration that begins when it is harvested. At home, most perishable food goes into the refrigerator, where the temperature hovers around forty degrees Fahrenheit. It probably will not be possible to keep your provisions at temperatures as low and as constant as in the refrigerator, so they are not going to last as long as they would at home. But with the help of insulation, evaporation, and cool sea water beneath the kayak's hull, you can stretch the food's life significantly.

Surface temperature of the ocean varies from place to place and with the time of year. For example, along the west coast of the United States the mean water temperature in June is around seventy-seven degrees at La Jolla, fifty-seven degrees at San Francisco, sixty degrees at Astoria (warmed by the Columbia River), fifty-three degrees at Seattle, and fifty degrees at Juneau. Perishables riding against the bottom of the boat can be cooled to these temperatures. (In the Sea of Cortez, winter water temperatures in the sixties and seventies at least keep your chocolate from melting.) Water temperature almost always is cooler than the air temperature by day, when you and your groceries would be on the water. A sleeping bag provides excellent insulation on top of perishables in the boat; unfurled over the food bags on shore, it can help them keep cool as you make camp and figure out the coolest place to keep them. In a hot, dry climate, spread wet towels over the bags to cool by evaporation. (The provisions will have to take what nature provides in the way of air temperature as they swing from a tree at night.)

## Meat, Poultry, and Fish

Ground meat, stew meat, poultry, and fish are the fresh foods with the shortest lives. At home, in the coldest part of the refrigerator, they last only one or two days. Roasts, steaks, and chops last longer—three to four days. The best way to carry all of them is frozen solid at the time you leave and wrapped in insulating packaging. Cook and eat them as soon as they become pliable. With reasonable care, prefrozen ground meat, stew meat, poultry and fish can be carried for twenty-four hours and the larger cuts of red meat for forty-eight. When you purchase any of those products fresh and unfrozen along the way, figure on using the most sensitive ones within the day and the steaks or chops tomorrow. You can tell when meat is going bad, as it develops an "off" smell and taste.

Meat and cheese from the supermarket's deli case last longer than fresh meat. Smoking extends the life of bacon, ham, sausages, and some lunch meat. So does vacuum packaging, which includes treatment to retard mold. Unopened, those will retain good quality in the refrigerator for at least a week. When kayaking, plan to open them within three or four days and to finish any leftovers within twenty-four hours of opening. Better to choose two or more small vacuum packages of these products than a single large one.

Eggs stay in top quality for two to four weeks at home. They keep best in the protective shells the hen provided for them. Keeping the shells unbroken is the obvious challenge while kayaking. Plan to use the eggs during the first week of your trip. Cooked eggs do not last as long as uncooked ones. Hard-boil in advance only those eggs you plan to eat the first day.

Dried meats that need no refrigeration include jerky, pepperoni, hard salami, and the like. To maximize their life, keep them frozen before departure and chilled while traveling. When they eventually begin to deteriorate they become moldy or slimy (like the half-eaten package of hot dogs that was forgotten and languished in the refrigerator for a couple of weeks). If that should happen (unlikely, unless an opened package gets wet), throw them out.

## Milk and Milk Products

Milk and the more fragile milk products such as cream cheese and cottage cheese are about as durable as the steaks. At home, they last for about a week. Butter, sour cream, and yogurt will keep twice as long. And all of these products go downhill more quickly once the container has been opened. With reasonable care, you can expect the delicate ones to last forty-eight hours and the hardier ones to last a week on a kayak trip. Milk that is going bad is readily identifiable by its awful taste. Butter becomes rancid (but it probably will be eaten or melt into a puddle before it gets to that point). Yogurt and sour cream warn you they are on the decline by developing an increasingly tangy taste.

Margarine (especially the soft kind sold in plastic tubs) and cheeses like Cheddar and Swiss have greater longevity. Many a tub of margarine has cruised the Inside Passage from end to end, spending six weeks in the process, and remained shipshape. Vacuum packaging helps keep cheese from molding. It will stay in good shape for at least a week. Wax-covered and foil-wrapped cheeses will last even longer.

## Fruits

Fruits and vegetables in the grocery store are kept cool by evaporation. Some of them do not even need that. They are good travelers, although prone to damage from crushing. Store fresh fruits uncovered whenever possible, and separated from the vegetables to maximize the longevity of both.

Most perishable are berries and cherries, which are best used within the first twenty-four hours of a trip. Less perishable are grapes, melons, pears, pineapple, and the stone fruits such as apricots, nectarines, peaches, and plums. Pineapple almost always is sold ripe and ready to eat; the others often can be purchased when they still have some ripening to do. That will extend their durability to just short of a week in many cases. The challenge is to keep them from being battered. Apples, oranges, and other citrus fruits last up to a month at home and will do almost as well on a trip.

## Vegetables

Vegetables include the most hardy travelers of all fresh foods. Like fruits, their longevity is extended by careful handling.

Most delicate of all is fresh corn on the cob. For peak enjoyment, carry it in the husk and cook it within twenty-four hours. There are few things more complementary to a clambake, fish fry, or grilled steak. Asparagus is the other tender traveler. It will wait for dinner the second night. Steam up a bunch to go with fresh salmon with lemon squeezed on top, and serve with big chunks of sturdy sourdough bread and fresh butter.

A bit more durable are broccoli, brussels sprouts, green peas (including snow peas) in the pod, green onions, rhubarb, and summer squash (including zucchini). That gives you the makings of a stir-fry well into a week-long trip. More durable yet, and likely to last the whole week, are artichokes, cabbage, carrots, cauliflower, celery, cucumbers, green beans, green peppers, lettuce (head lettuce more so than loose-leaf), and tomatoes. (Cherry tomatoes packed in their own plastic basket resist crushing best.)

Also a vegetable product is tofu, a high-protein soybean product that will outlast fresh meat, traveling for up to a week if kept in the sealed store container or in fresh, cool water in a zip locking bag. (Hard to find but ideal for kayaking is tofu packaged in a way that requires no refrigeration and lasts many months.) Cube it for stir-frying or crumble it into one-pot meals; its bland flavor takes on the taste of the other ingredients.

## Other Food

Breads treated with preservatives last longer than the others. Mold is their major enemy on a kayak trip. Fresh bread made without preservatives certainly will last several days, and other breads (unopened) can play backup after that. English muffins often last two weeks or longer.

I have never heard of a kayaker's peanut butter going rancid. Not so fresh nuts; they are much more perishable. To keep them tasty, either purchase them in airtight packages or pack them yourself in Seal-a-Meal bags. Try not to carry more than three days' worth in an opened package. (Tea and coffee benefit from the same treatment.)

Frozen food comes in handy at the beginning of a trip, as it helps keep perishables chilled while it is thawing. Frozen fruit juices and plain (unsauced) vegetables are good candidates. Use them as soon as they have thawed. Steer clear of the prepared dinners, entrées, and boil-in-the-bag vegetables plus sauce unless you can prepare them according to package directions. To do otherwise is to risk food poisoning. Likewise, do not carry from home prepared stock, gravy, or dishes containing meat, fish, poultry, eggs, or milk products. Instead, carry the ingredients and prepare the food in camp. Chill leftovers (just take the pot down to the water's edge, set it in and stir for a little while), keep them chilled, and use them within twenty-four hours. Rule of thumb is not to let any prepared food stand more than three hours at temperatures over forty degrees. For added protection, reheat and boil for ten minutes before eating. Food poisoning usually feels like the flu. Who needs that on an outdoor adventure? Although you may be the most thrifty user of leftovers at home, it may be much more prudent to discard them when you do not have a refrigerator in which to keep them cold.

# How Long Will It Last?

| Food | At Home | | On Kayak Trip | | | |
|---|---|---|---|---|---|---|
| | At room temperature | Refrigerated (40° F.) | Day | Weekend | Week | Longer |
| **Milk and milk products** | | | | | | |
| Milk | | 1 week | | X | | |
| Cottage cheese | | 1 week | | X | | |
| Cream cheese | | 1 week | | X | | |
| Butter | | 2 weeks | | | X | |
| Sour cream | | 2 weeks | | | X | |
| Yogurt | | 2 weeks | | | X | |
| Margarine | | 1 month | | | | X |
| Cheese | | 1 month | | | | X |
| **Meat, fish, and poultry** | | | | | | |
| Fish | | 1–2 days | X | | | |
| Poultry | | 1–2 days | X | | | |
| Ground meat | | 1–2 days | X | | | |
| Stew meat | | 1–2 days | X | | | |
| Steaks, chops | | 3–4 days | | X | | |
| Cured pork | | 1 week | | X | | |
| Lunch meat | | 1 week | | X | | |
| Eggs | | 2–4 weeks | | | X | |
| Dried meat (jerky) | 1 year | | | | | X |
| **Ripe fruit** | | | | | | |
| Berries | | 2–3 days | X | | | |
| Cherries | | 2–3 days | X | | | |
| Grapes | | 3–5 days | | X | | |
| Melons | | 3–5 days | | X | | |
| Pears | | 3–5 days | | X | | |
| Pineapple | | 3–5 days | | X | | |
| Stone fruits (apricots, nectarines, peaches, plums) | | 3–5 days | | X | | |
| Apples | | 1 month | | | | X |
| Citrus fruits (grapefruit, lemons, oranges, tangerines) | | 1 month | | | | X |
| Dried fruit | 6 months | | | | | X |

| Food | At Home | | On Kayak Trip | | | |
| --- | --- | --- | --- | --- | --- | --- |
| | At room temperature | Refrigerated (40° F.) | Day | Weekend | Week | Longer |
| **Ripe vegetables** | | | | | | |
| Corn | | 1 day | X | | | |
| Asparagus | | 2–3 days | | X | | |
| Broccoli, brussels sprouts, green peas, green onions, summer squash | | 3–5 days | | X | | |
| Tofu, artichokes, beets, cabbage, carrots, cauliflower, celery, cucumbers, green beans, green peppers, lettuce, tomatoes | | 1 week | | | X | |
| Potatoes, sweet potatoes, winter squash, dry onions | Several months at 50–60 degrees | | | | | X |
| Dried vegetables | 1 year | | | | | X |
| **Other foods** | | | | | | |
| Pies, pastries | | 2–3 days | | X | | |
| Bread | 1 week | | | X | | |
| Peanut butter | | 2 months | | | | X |
| Salad oil | 1–3 months | | | | | X |
| Mayonnaise | | 10–12 weeks | | | | X |
| Nuts, shelled | | 6 months | | | | X |
| Tea | 6 months | | | | | X |
| Coffee, instant | 6 months | | | | | X |
| Shortening, solid | 8 months | | | | | X |
| Coffee | 1 year | | | | | X |
| Tea, instant | 1 year | | | | | X |
| Bouillon | 1 year | | | | | X |
| Chocolate | 1 year | | | | | X |
| Honey, jam, syrup | 1 year | | | | | X |

Information on this chart is based on U.S. Department of Agriculture advice, interviews with Washington State University Cooperative Extension agents, and extensive experience with fresh foods on kayak trips in regions of temperate climate. The keeping times shown are intended as a guide to provisioning. Actual keeping time will vary with weather and handling.

# Provisioning for a Long Trip

What boggles the mind when confronting the task of provisioning for a long trip is the lack of a mental picture. How much food are we talking about? How many of us know how much we eat? When trying to lose weight, I can tell you about how many calories I consume in a day. When penny-pinching, I can tell you how much money I have to spend on food each week. People who shop once a week for the household groceries have a good idea of how high the grocery cart will be heaped and how many bags they will carry to the car. But how much food does it take to feed four people for a week, or two people for a month? Most of us draw a blank.

Provisioning starts with what you DO know—about how much you usually eat for breakfast, lunch, and dinner. For planning purposes, initially assume you are going to eat the same amount as you do on a typical day at home. We will do some rounding upward and add extra to accommodate the heartier appetite most people develop with all of that fresh air and exercise. (Trust me; no one with whom I have ever traveled has gone hungry, and I have always come back with food to spare.)

Provisioning also starts with what you like to eat. If you do not like instant oatmeal at home, you are not going to like it out there. You will eat the oatmeal if that is all there is to eat, but why put yourself in that position when there is so much to choose from that you DO like? This trip is supposed to be a pleasant experience; enjoyable food is part of it.

To avoid last-minute hassles and to let food-gathering fall comfortably into the rest of the trip preparations, I allow as much lead time as the duration of the trip. For a two-week trip, I start bringing home the groceries two weeks in advance. Earlier than that, I decide what I want to eat and how much of it I will need. During the off-season doldrums, I like to browse through cookbooks and collect ideas about good things to take paddling. Ingredients that are foreign to me or combinations that sound a little strange I would rather sample at home in advance. I make semiorganized master lists of ideas for things to eat. Then when a trip moves beyond the fantasizing to the planning stage, I take out the lists and have at hand a wealth of ideas for meals. If you are starting from scratch, look through the recipes in this book and list the ones you would like to try. Add to that old standbys and favorites, and you are on your way.

Next, take out a calendar and look at the dates of your trip. On each of those dates, write B, L, and D (for breakfast, lunch, and dinner). Now consult your itinerary. Let us say that you and your traveling companions are planning to meet after work Friday, drive to the town where you catch a ferry, stay there overnight, then board the ferry early the next morning for a two-hour ride and several hours' drive to the put-in point. Eating during that time is likely to be a combination of stops at McDonald's, a leisurely meal in the ferry's cafeteria, and munching in the car. Circle the letter for each meal you will be buying along the way. If you are going to stop at a farmers' market and buy picnic food just before lunch, circle that meal, too. In this way, follow your itinerary through the entire trip. When you are done you will have identified, by circling, each meal for which you will take money instead of food.

On month-long trips in Alaska and on the British Columbia coast, I often have been away from towns for a couple of weeks. When I get to a town, I am craving tortilla chips, cold beer, and a cheeseburger with lots of lettuce and tomatoes. I will want to eat nothing but fresh food in town, and take some along for the next day. Doing so varies the menu so I do not get bored with the traveling provisions.

Count all of the uncircled numbers you have left. You have just found out how many of each—breakfasts, lunches, and dinners—you will need to purchase in advance and pack. If more than one person will be bringing food, this is the point at which it is most convenient to divide responsibility for meals. For instance, each person in a group of four might bring the makings of two breakfasts, three lunches, and two dinners (or whatever combination adds up to the total you have figured you will need). This is starting to look manageable, right? And this is the point when it gets to be fun. Get out those lists of good things to eat and see how many of them you can include on this trip. (Of course you can have something more than once if you like!) I usually include at least two breakfasts and two dinners that are very quick to fix and a couple of new things we have never tried. The rest are favorite camp foods that range from "production numbers" to very simple fare. Include plenty of variety, and see "Food to Paddle On," for thoughts on menu-planning with nutrition in mind.

How much food makes a meal? As compared with eating at home, camp meals generally feature larger servings of fewer things. A typical breakfast might consist of fruit juice, hot cereal with milk, and coffee. Dinner might be a hearty chicken stew (with plenty of vegetables in with the chicken), hot biscuits, and cocoa laced with a little brandy. The fewer the courses, the simpler the equipment needed to cook and eat. To compensate for the absence of side dishes and trimmings, figure that each person will eat two city-size portions. (To feed four people hot cereal, prepare the amount the box says will serve eight.) And always round upward, taking the larger amount when the number of portions does not come out right.

Some people decide in advance what they are going to eat on each day, or assign kitchen duty along such lines as "Lisa and Tom cook Saturday, then Judy and Lee cook Sunday," etc. That works especially well when paddlers are sharing the challenge of fixing some fresh foods and some that keep a long time. Also, there is merit in having one person or team responsible for the menu for a whole day. That way, there will not be odd gaps or overlaps in the way the meals add up. But when going on an extended trip, I cannot anticipate what we are going to feel like eating on a certain day. So I just take food for "x" number of breakfasts and dinners, and decide day by day which of those appeals, or which will lend itself to preparation at the place we are camped. Some meals can be fixed with just a backpacker's stove; others want a campfire. Some are more appealing than others on cold or rainy days.

Armed with the information of how many meals I need to buy and what I might like to eat, I start grocery shopping and packaging the food as described in the chapter "Packing Down." The food I have bought is the food I will carry. That way, everyone is sharing the burden of carrying food (and has some in the boat in case they are separated from the rest of the group).

But what about food you might buy or gather or catch along the way? I wing it at reprovisioning points, giving little thought in advance to what I will buy. That decision will be dictated by what is available and what appeals to us at the time. I assume we will eat fresh food for the first twenty-four hours after leaving port, but what it will be I do not know.

In addition, there will be an element of surprise on those days when we feast on the bounty of sea and shore. I have never gone on a trip where there was not at least a degree of success fishing and foraging, so some of the meals I plan are based on that. I take all of the makings for bouillabaisse, figuring we will find the fish and shellfish ingredients. But I also take a backup meal (something as simple as ramen-type noodle dinners) just in case there is no fish to be found. I have never had to fall back on these extra meals, but the food often has come in handy for stretching provisions to accommodate dinner guests or as emergency fare in case we are weathered in and cannot get back for a couple of extra days. The spare food also lets you satisfy any ravenous appetites that catch you by surprise.

All of the food does not need to go with you for the entire trip. It makes the boats easier to pack and keeps food in better shape if you carry what you need for each leg of the trip and pick up a new batch of provisions at one or two points along the way. This is especially appropriate on trips of more than a couple of weeks; food that has been traveling that long starts to get pretty tired, and some bags may start to leak. So how do you cache food along the way? Mail it to yourself. Pack a box of food that will keep and send it care of the postmaster in a port where you plan to call. Write on the box that you are traveling in the area and expect to arrive on a particular date. Add "If not claimed by [later date], please forward to..." or "return to sender."

Audrey Sutherland of Hawaii has used this system extensively in her traveling in remote parts of Alaska. She always packs some strapping tape in the box. When she picks it up, she takes out the food and then refills the box with charts and maps with which she is finished, souvenirs she has picked up along the way, and any gear she no longer needs. Then she tapes up the box and mails it back to her home address.

The only trouble I have had with this system has been the delay in clearing customs when things are sent from the United States into Canada. Customs often takes two weeks or more. In one case, a package I mailed took nine months to arrive! The way to avoid a delay is to mark the box "Merchandise" or "Gift." Better yet, if you are going into Canada to start your trip, mail your boxes of provisions after you are over the border.

Finally, there is the question of water. Figure that each person will consume one gallon a day through drinking and in food. Charts and topographic maps indicate streams and other sources of water, but it is always wise to check with local authorities to find out if weather or other conditions have dried up the supply. Assume you can get water in any settlement. In a pinch, you can ask for a little from fishboats or pleasure craft. But take enough water bags or other containers to keep you in water from point to point, and minimize your need of it by using sea water for cooking and washing whenever possible.

# Food Drying

Drying some of your favorite foods at home makes for superior eating on kayak trips of more than a couple of days. Dried foods can greatly improve and vary the menu on an extended trip. They keep for months—in some cases, for more than a year—without refrigeration. That can greatly extend your paddling time and range. Dried foods are compact and lightweight for easy packing. Drying gives you foods you really enjoy, extending the limits of products you can buy.

A succulent slice of beef jerky flavored with burgundy, and without the overpowering salt of store-bought jerkies, is just one of the treats you can have on hand. A little dried rhubarb perks up the flavor of warm fruit compote or cobbler while naturally thickening the sauce. An elegant stroganoff made from scratch is ready to serve within minutes of paddling into camp— because you made a big batch of it at home, and dried a few servings for the ultimate in convenience food.

You can eat much better fare than commercially freeze-dried foods at a fraction of the price through simple drying projects that do not require more than basic kitchen skills. (If you can measure ingredients, cut things into smaller pieces, and set a thermostat, you have what it takes.)

A home oven, cookie sheet, and some plastic wrap are all the equipment required. Beyond that, options range from screens for drying foods in the sun and homemade box devices that do the job with light bulb heat to food-drying appliances priced from seventy-five dollars on up into three figures—starting with the number three. The whole thing can be as high-tech or as simple and in-harmony-with-nature as you like.

A reasonable place to start food drying is with a batch of Tomato Sauce Leather or Dried Apple Sauce in the oven—maybe both at the same time. Then borrow a friend's food dryer, either homemade or manufactured, to see how it compares in convenience and energy use. Many paddlers find year-round food drying to be a pleasant complementary activity. They are the best candidates for building or buying a dryer of their own. For those who dry food once or twice a year when preparing for a trip, borrowing or co-owning a dryer may make more sense.

The idea is to extract water, which will reduce the food's volume to one-third to one-tenth of original size, and the weight correspondingly. In some cases, the dried food itself is the end product—as in making fruit leather or beef jerky, both delicious and easy to carry for lunch and snacks. In other cases the food is rehydrated in camp by soaking or cooking in fresh water. In minutes, a dark red leather turns into fragrant tomato sauce or a crumbly powder becomes crispy corned beef hash.

Drying preserves the color, flavor, and nutritional value of foods. Temperatures used are low compared to oven heat, ideally ranging from around 90 to about 150 degrees Fahrenheit. Vegetables and fruit dry best at the lower temperatures and meats and main dishes in the higher range. Commercially made food dryers let you adjust the temperature in relation to the food being dried. When using the oven, simply set the temperature as low as possible (usually between 150 and 200 degrees). An oven is less energy-efficient than a food dryer, and it takes some experimenting to discover how much time is needed.

Drying time varies according to such factors as the thickness of the food being dried, its moisture content, and the humidity and circulation of the surrounding air. Many foods dry in eight hours or a little longer, making it easy to do a batch overnight or while away at work during the day. (When our food dryer starts running around the clock, day after day, Hazel, the cat, retreats under the bed to sulk, knowing that her people are about to leave her to go kayaking.)

As each batch of food is dried, it needs to be sealed airtight. Seal-A-Meal bags make an easy job of it. Meal-size portions or small batches of food like jerky can be sealed in impermeable packages to be opened one at a time. This provides good protection against food getting wet: if one bag springs a leak, the rest of the food remains dry. Contents of a sealed bag always can be dumped into a zip locking bag for repeated opening and closing.

## Tomato Sauce Leather

One of the most useful things to have on hand for cooking in camp is tomato sauce. An eight-ounce can of it weighs, of course, eight ounces—not including the extra weight of the can. Dried at home, that same tomato sauce weighs between one and two ounces, and there is no can to pack out.

To dry tomato sauce into leather using a home oven, pour the contents of an eight-ounce can onto plastic wrap on a cookie sheet. Spread the sauce into a circle about one-fourth inch deep at the edge and a little thinner in the center, where it dries more slowly. The puddle of tomato sauce will be about the diameter of a dinner plate. You can make two batches on a big cookie sheet.

Set the oven temperature as low as possible and prop open the door a few inches to allow moisture to escape. (A wooden mixing spoon works well as a prop.) Dry until the center is no longer sticky and the edges peel readily from the plastic, approximately eight hours. While leather is still warm from the oven, roll it up in the same piece of plastic on which it was dried.

As an alternative, peel the warm leather from the plastic to cool, then pulverize it in a blender to make a little pile of pink powder about the size of a golf ball. Pour it into a plastic sandwich bag and seal with a twist-tie.

To reconstitute leather, tear it into pieces of postage stamp size and drop into one cup boiling water. Let it soak for about twenty minutes, stirring occasionally. Simmer and stir, if necessary, to finish smoothing it out.

To speed reconstitution at dinner time, presoak the leather during the day in a cup of water. (Just put the water and bits of leather into a small poly bottle, cap it and stow in the boat.) Pour the contents into a small pot and simmer for a few minutes to finish the job.

Powdered leather reconstitutes almost instantly when boiling water is stirred into it.

To improve the flavor of canned tomato sauce, add one tablespoon red wine and a sprinkling of herbs of your choice to the sauce before drying, or start with homemade tomato sauce.

## Fruit Leathers

In a blender, purée pieces of any fresh fruit and/or berries, adding a little water or fruit juice as needed to create a mixture that is pourable, but not runny. Any combination that tastes good in the blender will taste just as good or better as a leather. Experiment with adding lemon juice, cinnamon, frozen fruit juice concentrate (for sweetening), chopped nuts, or unsalted sunflower seeds.

Pour onto plastic-lined cookie sheet and dry according to instructions for Tomato Sauce Leather. One cup of fruit purée makes one roll of leather, an individual serving to nibble for lunch or a snack. Also use bits of fruit leather in place of jelly, sprinkle them on hot cereal, or mix into granola.

## Dried Apple Sauce

Pour canned or homemade apple sauce by cupfuls onto plastic sheets. Dry into leather for carrying, and reconstitute in camp just as you would Tomato Sauce Leather.

## Dried Fresh Fruits

Drying your own fruit costs less (by about half) than buying fruit already dried. It also gives you greater variety. Banana chips for snacking, dried blueberries and bits of nectarine to add to a gorp-type trail mix, and chopped rhubarb to use in fruit compote are a few of the possibilities.

For good results, use only ripe fruit in perfect condition. (Less-than-perfect fruits and pieces work beautifully in fruit leathers, but not on their own.) Wash the fruit well and slice as evenly as the shape of the fruit allows. Edible skins add flavor, color, and food value to dried fruits.

No further preparation is needed unless you wish to prevent some darkening of apples, pears, and other fruits that turn brown when exposed to air. If so, dip the cut pieces in lemon or orange juice before laying them on drying racks or trays.

The amount of time needed for drying in the oven ranges from overnight to twenty-four hours or more (for thick pineapple chunks). The finished product should be leathery. A final twenty minutes of actual baking at 175 degrees will kill any microorganisms that may have survived the drying process and could shorten storage life. Cool and store in airtight containers.

Most dried fruit is eaten dry or simmered with fresh water to serve in warm sauces, compotes, cobblers, or "fruit soup."

## Home-dried Tomatoes

When tomatoes are plentiful and ripe, slice them one-fourth-inch thick and dry, turning at least once. These may take as long as twenty-four hours because tomatoes contain so much water. Drying time is speeded if the slices are dried on a rack through which air can circulate. In the oven, you can use a cake-cooling rack on a cookie sheet or a broiler pan with rack.

Plain, dried tomato slices make excellent snacking, rich in vitamin C. And they are easy to use in cooking. Simply stir them into one-pot meals or layer them into casseroles without presoaking. In just a few minutes, they will reconstitute to add the incomparable flavor of fresh tomato to your meal.

You will not believe how compact tomatoes become: twenty-five pounds of them dries into a bagful weighing just one to two pounds.

## Dried Frozen Vegetables

Packing an assortment of vegetables, lightweight and in little space, is easy when you combine the convenience of frozen vegetables from the grocery store with home food drying. Starting with fresh vegetables would require the initial step of blanching—immersing briefly in boiling water, or steaming—before drying. But the frozen vegetables already have been blanched.

We frequently dry frozen whole-kernel corn, cut green beans, mixed vegetables, broccoli, and cauliflower with very good results. The cauliflower turns a discouraging shade of brown when dried. Do not be concerned; it whitens again when reconstituted. Simply spread the frozen vegetables on a drying rack as you would when dehydrating sliced tomatoes. Cut any large chunks to about the same thickness as the rest of the pieces. They will take about eight hours to dry in the oven.

The easiest way to reconstitute dried vegetables is to pour boiling water on them, then set them aside to soak while you prepare the rest of the meal. Put the vegetables on the fire to finish cooking for a few minutes, or stir the soaked vegetables into a one-pot meal for the final minutes of simmering.

Unfortunately, frozen snow peas do not dry well. The dried pods become so papery and brittle that they end up as little more than dust. Reconstituted, they have little of the flavor and none of the texture that makes snow peas such a pleasure in stir-fries and all kinds of Oriental dishes.

## Dried Fresh Vegetables

Starting with fresh vegetables instead of frozen ones requires a preliminary step that gives you a much better dried product in terms of color, flavor, and nutrition. Just before drying, steam the washed, sliced vegetables for one to twenty minutes, until the edges become translucent. Shredded cabbage and chopped spinach take the minimum time; carrots may need the maximum, depending upon how thickly they are sliced.

A few vegetables—including some of those most often carried by kayakers—do not need the preliminary steam treatment. They include tomatoes, onions, green peppers, and mushrooms.

Spread the prepared vegetables on racks and dry until hard or crisp. Drying time ranges from a few hours for herbs to twenty-four hours or more for the most dense vegetables. Cool and pack in airtight containers.

To reconstitute, soak in fresh water. Using hot water or simmering speeds the process. I usually pour boiling water over dried vegetables and let them stand a few minutes (until they have returned to normal size), before adding them to a pot of ingredients. That seems to minimize cooking time and fuel consumption while assuring that the dried ingredients reconstitute completely.

Any dried vegetable can be reconstituted in cold water; it just takes more time. Shredded cabbage and similar salad ingredients come back to life in just a few minutes. Others may take hours. Put them into a poly bottle and let them soak all day for speedy preparation at dinner time.

## Dried Mexican-style Chilies

Mexican dishes sparkle with the distinctive flavor of mild, green chilies. Widely sold in cans, they are easy to dry. Buy whole, not diced chilies for ease in handling. Rinse off any seeds, then spread the chilies flat on a cookie sheet or rack. Dry until brittle, about eight hours. The peppers do not need to be reconstituted separately; just add them dried.

## Dried Black Olives

Easier to handle and more distinctive than chopped or sliced olives are pitted whole ones, cut in half lengthwise. Spread them, cut-side down, on a cookie sheet or rack and dry for about ten hours, turning once. The funny-looking little black pellets that result will reconstitute when added to spaghetti sauce, tamale pie, or the like, adding texture as well as flavor and color.

## Yogurt Drops

Fresh milk products are difficult to carry, and many kayakers start craving them. A pleasant, sweet snack that satisfies that desire with real yogurt is a handful of home-dried yogurt drops.

Start with either homemade or store-bought yogurt, plain or the flavored kind (but not the varieties that have jamlike fruit in the bottom of
the container). Lemon, strawberry, piña colada, and coffee flavors are
among my favorites for drying. Drop yogurt by half-teaspoonfuls onto
plastic wrap and dry for about eight hours. An eight-ounce carton of yogurt will make about 150 drops. Carry them for snacks or lunch.

## Dried Grated Cheese

Fresh Cheddar cheese will dry beautifully. Grate or shred it and
spread in a single layer on two or more paper towels. Change the paper
as it absorbs oil from the cheese. It may take twelve or more hours for
the cheese to dry to the point where no more oil comes out. Crumble the
dry cheese into a plastic bag for carrying. Sprinkle it on top of casseroles
and chili, stir it into macaroni, roll it into burritos or enchiladas, make
cheese sauce from it.

Theoretically one should be able to shred and dry Monterey jack
cheese in the same way. I have yet to succeed at this, as the cheese becomes permanently soldered to the paper toweling. The paper seems to
disappear into casseroles to which I add the cheese, with no untoward
effects. However, I neither consider this a culinary success nor recommend replication.

## Precooked Meals

There are few long-distance kayakers who eat gourmet fare to
match that carried by Audrey Sutherland of Hawaii. This paddling
grandmother, who travels solo for weeks and months at a time, makes
big batches of stew, stroganoff, and other hearty main dishes at home.
Then she dries single servings and packs them to take on her trips.

For best results, cut chunks of meat and vegetables down to bite size
before drying the food for about eight hours, until uniformly dry. Crumble into plastic bags and seal. In camp, add enough water to replace that
removed in drying: soak and heat for about thirty minutes to reconstitute.

## Corned Beef Hash

One of our favorite hearty camp breakfasts is crisp-fried corned beef
hash served with English muffins. The hash comes out of a can at home
many weeks in advance. We buy it on sale and dry it on paper towels to

absorb grease. Usually the paper needs to be replaced two or three times. Rejoice while replacing it; every bit of grease that comes out will give the hash longer life. (I have cooked home-dried hash a year after drying and found it to be excellent. However, most food-drying guides recommend that home-dried meat products be used within three months if they are being stored at room temperature. I stretch that by keeping the packets of dried hash in the freezer until it is time to take them paddling.

Dry the hash for about ten hours, until no more grease comes out. To reconstitute, crumble it into a skillet and add water, bit by bit, stirring over heat. Soon it will look and smell as if it had never been dried—except, of course, there is not enough grease left in it to brown properly. Add a tablespoon of oil or margarine after the hash has fully reconstituted, and it will fry up crispy and brown. Total time for reconstituting and cooking is about twenty minutes.

## Other Canned Foods

Many foods that come in cans are easy to dry at home, making them much more compact and less weighty. In reading about tomato sauce, green chilies, black olives, and corned beef hash, you surely have thought of other possibilities. Indeed, they are legion. Baked beans, refried beans, chili, beef stew, spaghetti sauce, and similar canned foods are easy to dry. When reconstituted, they cannot be distinguished from the same product from a just-opened can.

Among the canned foods I have dried with success are Mexican-style refried beans, chili with beef and beans, enchilada sauce, cut green beans, both whole kernel and cream-style corn, applesauce, and crushed pineapple. Although I have not tried drying canned tuna, I am told that it works well if you choose the kind that is packed in water (not oil) and drain off the water before drying. Then break the tuna into flakes of similar size.

Canned foods do not require pretreatment. Simply spread them evenly on the drying tray. Line the tray with plastic wrap if the food is runny or sticky. Line the tray with paper towels if the food contains oil that will be released as the product dries. Cut or break up any large chunks, either in advance or when you discover that they are drying more slowly than the rest. Drying time ranges from overnight to more than twenty-four hours. (The times given for tomato sauce, olives, and corned beef hash will give you an idea of how long foods of similar density need to dry.) Cool and store in airtight containers.

To reconstitute, add fresh water and simmer until the food is hot and as moist as you like it. Usually, it takes equal amounts of fresh water and dried food.

# Dried Sausages

Wonderful with breakfast pancakes or mixed into a batch of scalloped potatoes at dinner time are home-dried sausages. Start with a package of fully precooked, skinless sausages from the supermarket freezer case. (Brown 'n' Serve is one commonly sold brand. Find it, and you will know you are in the right department.)

Place whole sausages or slices on at least three layers of paper towels and dry for about eighteen hours, changing the paper frequently, squeezing out and patting off as much grease as possible. The sausages will never become completely dry; they are ready to travel when the paper under them in the dryer remains grease free. Seal in plastic bags and keep in the freezer until packing to leave. Shelf life at room temperature is about six weeks.

To reconstitute, place in skillet with a little water and simmer, adding water until sausage has regained its plumpness—about twenty minutes. Add about one tablespoon oil or margarine and fry to brown.

# Beef Jerky

Jerky is meat preserved by marinating and drying. It is a very concentrated form of protein, delicious for munching "as is" and a welcome addition to one-pot meals. Almost every recipe book advises starting with flank steak. Rubbish! Use round steak (whole, top, or bottom), which costs half as much. You will not be able to tell the difference after the marinade and drying have worked their magic on flavor and texture. Choose the leanest cuts of meat, those with a minimum of fat marbling.

Slicing the meat is easy with a serrated knife intended for slicing ham, frozen foods, or bread. And the skittish meat is more cooperative if it is half frozen (or half thawed, depending upon your perspective). Slice across the grain for a more tender jerky; slice with the grain to make it more chewy. Trim off and discard as much fat as possible.

Place meat in marinade to cover and refrigerate at least two hours. I usually marinate the meat overnight, then put it into the dryer the next morning and ignore it all day. During the evening I turn the slices occasionally and test for dryness. The jerky is done by bedtime. To test for doneness, remove a piece of meat and let it cool to room temperature, then bend. It should be pliable, much like green willow, when done. (No, it does not get as brittle as the jerky sold in stores.) Cool and seal in plastic bags. Store in freezer until time to leave. It should be good to eat for at least three months unrefrigerated. We would not know; ours never lasts that long at the rate we nibble on it.

See "Recipes" for several flavors of marinade to use in making beef jerky, and for instructions on making your own quick-cooking rice. And if food-drying appeals to you, there are many excellent books on the subject; two of my favorites are listed under "Related Reading."

# Dried Ingredients—How Much to Use?

**Dry Milk Powder:**
⅟₄ cup dry milk powder plus scant cup water makes 1 cup milk.
1 cup dry milk powder plus scant quart water makes 1 quart milk.

**Powdered Eggs:**
2 tablespoons dry egg powder plus 1 tablespoon water is equivalent to 1 egg.
¾ cup (12 tablespoons) egg powder plus ⅓ cup water makes enough scrambled eggs or omelet to serve 2.

**Dried Fruits:**
½ cup dried fruit plus ½ cup water makes 1 serving dried fruit (about 1 cup cooked fruit). Some dried fruits, especially the softer ones such as commercially dried prunes and apricots, do not swell as much as do home-dried fruits. When using the softer ones in cooking, add a little extra fruit (1 or 2 pieces per serving).

**Dried Vegetables:**
½ cup dried vegetables plus ½ cup water makes 1 serving (about 1 cup cooked vegetables). Some vegetables require a little more water; add as needed.

**Butter Buds:**
1 packet Butter Buds plus ½ cup water makes ½ cup butter flavored liquid, enough to season 2 to 4 servings of food.

[Continued on p. 72]

**Rice:**
⅓ cup raw white or brown rice plus ⅔ cup water makes 1 cup cooked rice.

When using processed (instant or fast-cooking) rice, follow package directions.

**Beans, Peas, Lentils:**
½ pound (about 1 cup) dry beans, peas, or lentils soaked and simmered in as much water as the dry product will absorb (at least 4 cups) makes 3 to 4 cups cooked.

**Pasta:**
3 to 4 ounces (1 cup) dry pasta cooked in at least 6 cups water (enough to let pasta boil freely) makes about 2 cups cooked pasta.

**Cereal:**
⅓ cup oatmeal, cracked wheat, or other unprocessed cereal plus 1 cup water makes 1 serving cooked cereal.

When using processed (instant or fast-cooking) cereal, follow package directions.

# Traveling with Sourdough

Sourdough is simple stuff. A staple of frontier cookery, it traveled throughout the North American wilderness in trappers' packs and traders' canoes. So why not take it along on a kayak trip?

All that a sourdough "starter" requires is occasional feeding with flour and water (which it gets every time you cook with it) and shelter from extremes of cold or heat. Give it those things and keep it in plastic (it interacts with metal, to the detriment of both) and sourdough goes paddling just fine.

Why use sourdough? It replaces yeast and other ingredients that make foods rise. With it, you can turn out pancakes, biscuits, breads, desserts, and more. Each will have at least a trace of the popular sourdough taste. And, in addition, foods thus made provide extra protein.

Only a cup of sourdough starter needs to be carried. I keep mine in a screw-top plastic jar, tightening the top before getting under way. This, of course, is heresy to sourdough purists, who insist that starter should never be capped tight. There is reason for that. Sourdough makes baked goods rise because it contains wild yeasts. It gathers those wild yeasts from the air.

Sourdough also expands—rapidly and dramatically—when shaken or exposed to heat. Picture a surf-landing on a sandy beach. Picture a kayak pulled up on the sand while paddlers go beachcombing and picnicking in the sun. Picture returning to the boat to find the rear hatch burping, and beneath that hatch, sourdough engulfing gear like The Blob in the science fiction film.

This does not happen when sourdough starter travels in a container with a top sealed tight. It can (and did) happen when using a margarine tub with a snap-on lid.

My favorite screw-top "sourdough pot" holds about two cups. That capacity gives the cup of starter enough headroom to double in bulk in response to jostling or heat. Theoretically, a securely capped container could explode. Sourdough literature includes apocrypha about starter "blowing up" in the baggage compartments of aircraft. (The solemn conclusion is that a person should not carry a breakable container of sourdough in a suitcase—and I certainly would hesitate to travel with a kayaker doing so.)

But my tight-capped container has not detonated in many miles of travel in a temperate climate zone. Neither has my sourdough shown any adverse effects from being cooped up for several hours a day. Unscrewing the cap to rest loosely in camp has kept the starter and its wild yeasts working.

Frontiersmen up north used to carry sourdough starter in an empty tobacco can, tucking it into a pocket to be kept warm by body heat. They even slept with it at night. Freezing inactivates the enzymes that make the sourdough work, and chilling slows them noticeably. Sourdough works best at temperatures between sixty and eighty degrees Fahrenheit. After it has had eight hours in that range to "digest" a feeding, the starter can be kept cooler, down to around thirty-five degrees. To optimize its performance, protect a starter from extremes of temperature beyond that range.

When paddling in icy water, you may want to put something between your sourdough container and the bottom of the boat. Otherwise, that is the perfect place to keep the stuff at a constant temperature in the zone it likes. On top of it, put an insulating layer of gear to shield the sourdough from sun beating down on the deck. (In pack train and chuck-wagon, sourdough was protected from heat by burying the starter in the flour sack.)

Flour, salt, cornmeal, and other ingredients for making assorted sourdough treats can be plastic-bagged in appropriate quantities. All of the bags then go into a plastic mixing bowl with a snap-on lid. I shortened the handle of a wooden spoon so it fits inside the bowl, too. And for good measure (literally), I toss in a plastic half-cup measure and a set of measuring spoons. Then everything that goes with the sourdough is packed together in the mixing bowl.

If this sounds like a hassle, remember that a sourdough starter and its attendant staples go in place of—not in addition to—an assortment of mixes with which to make pancakes, biscuits, and other breads. On some trips you can travel with Betty Crocker, Aunt Jemima, Duncan Hines, and company. On other trips, bake "from scratch" with sourdough.

At home, your sourdough pot will contain about two cups. When packing for a kayak trip, take half of it. When preparing to bake in camp, dump all of it into the mixing bowl and feed it overnight as described in the sourdough starter recipe, following. Next day, skim off a cup to carry; bake with the rest.

Do not wash the traveling sourdough jar while it is virtually empty. As a matter of fact, it is smart not to scrape it clean. Why? Because if something should destroy the batch "feeding" overnight, there will be enough clinging to the "empty" container to get a new batch going. (Add enough flour to equal the amount of leftovers and stir in the same amount of water. Repeat every six to eight hours until you have a full cup again.)

I have never heard of a wild animal being attracted to the sour smell of working sourdough. However, the safest place for it at night is with the rest of the provisions, hanging in a tree. A string-mesh bag and a length of parachute cord make it easy to hoist the foil-capped mixing bowl separately, or just set the bowl carefully atop other food before cinching the drawstring of a stuff sack.

## Sourdough Starter

There are many recipes for starter. This one is my favorite—for flavor and dependability.

1 potato
2 cups water
3 tablespoons sugar (divided)
2 cups plus 2 tablespoons flour

Scrub the potato, cut it in chunks, and simmer in water until soft. Cool. Discard potato skin. Beat into a lump-free purée. Measure, adding water as needed to make 2 cups.

[Continued on p. 76]

Stir in 2 tablespoons of the sugar. Add 2 cups flour in small amounts, beating well to blend.

Sterilize a 1-quart glass jar or ceramic crock. Pour in batter, cover loosely with foil and allow to stand at room temperature. After about three days, the mixture will begin to "work," bubbling throughout. Encourage it by adding the additional 1 tablespoon sugar and 2 tablespoons flour, stirring well. Add water, if needed, to give the mixture the consistency of thick batter (pourable, but not runny).

The starter will respond with a 24-hour display of bubbling exuberance, then settle down. Let it keep aging at room temperature, stirring daily, for the remainder of a week. You now have a starter that is ready to use. Or, for a more distinctly sour flavor, stir daily and let it age for another week.

Keep sourdough starter at room temperature when using it often, two or more times a week. When using it just once a week or less frequently than that, put it in the refrigerator. Keep it loosely capped; foil works just fine for that.

To remain active, the starter needs feeding at least once a week. In a large mixing bowl, combine

1 cup starter
1 cup flour
1 scant cup warm water

Beat together with a wooden spoon. Cover bowl loosely and leave it at room temperature overnight. The next morning, take out 1 cup of the mixture and stir it into the old starter. That replaces the cupful borrowed the previous night and rejuvenates the perennial pot.

The remainder in the mixing bowl is ready for baking (or to discard if this is a morning when you do not want to bake). There should be about a cupful of it. All of the recipes in this book using sourdough start with that amount. If you are looking at a visibly skimpy cupful of sourdough "sponge" in the bowl, borrow additional sourdough from the stirred-together mixture in the pot, but always leave at least one full cup in there.

# Fishing and Foraging

My paddling partner had gone to explore the Southeast Alaska bay we had paddled into the previous night. I opted for checking out the surroundings of our campsite, used many times over the years by boat-weary crews of salmon trollers who anchored nearby. Following a stream to find the best place to dip water, I found a bonus in a cool, deep pool—a six-pack of beer that had been chilling for about a year, judging from the algae on the cans. Leaving it in the "cooler" for the moment, I headed for the sunny bank at the edge of the woods. There, salmonberries ripened in abundance. In no time at all I half-filled a cooking pot with the choicest, reddest ones.

Then I saw Randy's kayak heading for our beach. I hollered and waved. In response, he lifted a clear plastic bag from the cockpit. Clearly silhouetted in it was a big fish. He had encountered a fishboat on the way to sell its catch at a fish-buying scow, and purchased a beautiful, fresh-caught salmon for dinner. We would feast on salmon poached in beer (none the worse for its long wait), and berry-studded muffins. Most of the meal had all but fallen into our hands.

That, of course, is not typical of kayakers' everyday fishing and foraging. Often, traveling and sightseeing leave no time to search for edibles elsewhere than in the food bags. On other occasions, when paddlers have time and inclination, wild edibles decline to be found. Living off the land while kayaking is an appealing, romantic notion that does not match reality. It adds a delightful dimension to sea kayaking and, as recreation, would be a shame to miss. But the time involved and the limited scope of what is available at a particular time make it impractical as a key source of food. I forage for fun and consider anything that it brings to mealtime as frosting on the cake. (And the basics of harvesting simple wild foods are good to know in case of emergency.)

This chapter's goal is to introduce some of the wild edibles most common to the saltwater coastal environment. Excellent field guides (listed in "Related Reading") provide details for those who wish to try some fishing or foraging, best done with a companion who has first-hand knowledge of the local scene.

# Fish

**Rockfish.** If there were not photos to prove it, no one would believe the story of Randy's being caught by a fish. He was jigging for rockfish from a single kayak when I heard him call. There he sat with his right arm as high in the air as he could hold it. Just below his hand was the mouth of a lingcod so big the tip of its tail was still in the water. Each time Randy tried to give the fish a rap on the head, the tail would touch the boat and the fish would leap to life, almost upsetting the boat. As I quickly snapped two photos, we debated how to land the monster without a net. But it was the fish that took decisive action. As Randy's arm sagged from the weight the powerful tail pushed off the deck, and in a soaring arc that dislodged the hook the big cod leaped free.

That is about as exciting as it gets fishing for rockfish with a hand-line, an activity scorned by sophisticated anglers who challenge more sporty fish—and loved by those whose primary goal is to catch something to eat. The rockfish, including, cod, cabezon, greenling, lingcod, Pacific cod, red snapper, and rock cod, all make excellent eating. Try chunks of fish dipped in tempura batter and deep-fried, wrap fillets in foil to steam along with vegetables, or stir bite-size pieces into chowders.

Rockfish congregate in schools near the bottom of kelp beds (good anchorage for a kayak in current or wind) and along steep, rocky shorelines, especially where there is an underwater point. They are most likely to be found where the water is thirty to forty feet deep.

Jigging gear is the simplest of fishing tackle. All you need is a lead weight, a bottom-fishing lure on one hundred feet of sixty-pound-test monofilament line, and something to wind it on. (An empty aluminum beverage can works fine.) Lower the lure to the bottom, then raise it about three feet and let it flutter down a couple of feet. Repeat the action several times. If nothing happens, retrieve the line with a stop-start motion that may attract something on the way up. If you think you have a nibble, jerk hard to set the hook. If nothing happens after a few repetitions, assume that nobody is home down there and try another spot.

Rap a fish smartly on the head upon bringing it into the boat, using a short piece of driftwood as a "fish bonker." Either fillet the catch on the spot or tie it to the deck, giving it protection from the sun. Rockfish are very perishable and should be cleaned as soon as possible. To fillet, lay the fish on its side and cut downward just behind the gills until the knife hits the backbone. (The scrunching sound is the knife cutting through the rib cage.) Then start at the tail and slide the knife forward along the backbone until you reach the first cut and can lift off the whole fillet. Turn the fish over and do the same on the other side. Discard all but the two fillets. Place each of them skin side down and, starting at the tail end, slide the knife along between skin and meat. Discard the skin. Cut away and discard the rib cage.

**Salmon.** Salmon are the prize catch of Northwest waters from Alaska to the mouth of the Columbia. Going after them (or almost anything other than rockfish) requires a rod and reel. Most kayakers fish for salmon either by trolling (trailing a line behind the boat as they paddle) or drift-fishing (letting the boat drift while casting out or jigging straight down with a weighted lure). Trolling is easiest from a double kayak or a single with a deck-mounted bracket for the rod.

Unlike the rockfish that simply hang from the hook as you hold them aloft, these are fighting fish. You will need a landing net. Recommended tackle includes a rod between seven and ten feet long, a heavy-duty saltwater spinning reel for casting (either a single action reel or a star drag multiplying reel works fine for jigging), and twenty-pound-test monofilament line. For best results, use a flasher and hoochie.

If you are still following this with interest, you (a) need no further advice, and/or (b) should consult a local tackle shop. There are many avid kayak anglers, some for whom the kayak offers just the newest challenge in a lifelong pursuit of game fish. I know of two kayaks equipped with depth sounders for fish-finding. But my interest and expertise lie in the cooking rather than in the catching. Bring me a salmon and I will either fillet it as outlined above or clean it (cutting off head and tail), wrap the whole fish in foil, and roast. For details, see "Recipes." Instructions for baking a salmon Indian-style are on p. 80.

# Indian-style Salmon Bake

Natives of the Pacific Northwest paddled its coastal waters, caught its salmon, and cooked their catch with skills that the new generation of sea kayakers finds especially intriguing. In the old techniques, there is much that can be used today. Baking a fresh-caught salmon beside a beach fire is the highlight of many a kayak trip.

"Keep it simple," advises Lee Moyer of Pacific Water Sports, as he shares his favorite way of preparing salmon. It is patterned after the traditional Indian technique:

Clean the salmon, cutting the meat away from the bones into a butterfly fillet. Leave skin intact.

Split a four-foot pole or branch from one end to about the mid-point. Lay the salmon fillet in the split, supporting it with four or five crosspieces of split wood, each about one foot long. Place crosspieces alternately in front and in back of the fillet.

Wrap wire around the pole just above and just below the salmon, squeezing tight the split to hold the fish in place.

Build a hot fire and place the end of the pole in the ground to hold the fleshy side of the fillet toward the flames. For best results, cook slowly while minimizing exposure to smoke. And for best flavor, burn hardwood rather than the more resinous softwoods.

# Crabs and Shrimp

**Crabs.** Crabs inhabit all the oceans of the world and scuttle across all kinds of bottoms—rock, gravel, sand, and mud. At low tide they can be found in tide pools, buried in sand, or hiding under seaweed. You can catch them by hand on shore and with a dip net in shallow water. When the tide is out, paddle in the shallows scouting for them on the bottom. (Polarized sunglasses help you see through surface glare.) Scoop the net under the crab and quickly lift it out of the water. Then grab it by the rear legs and hold upright or grasp at the rear of the shell with thumb and fingers.

Folding crab traps are more effective. At least two models are sold with kayakers in mind. To catch the big Dungeness crabs of the Pacific coast, follow the example of commercial crabbers who set traps for them just offshore of breaking surf in thirty to fifty feet of water. Other prime places are near long sandy spits, off river mouths, or in inside waters with sandy bottoms and eelgrass. Use fresh bait, such as clams and fish scraps. The best time for trapping is at the slack because crabs like to feed when there is no current. Line up the trap entrance with the current flow and mark it with a float you can readily identify. Check the trap every hour or leave it out overnight.

Most jurisdictions prohibit the taking of female Dungeness crabs (which have a much broader plate on the underside between the legs than do males) and any crabs that measure less than six inches wide. (Check local regulations for details.) Put the keepers in a wet burlap sack or something else that will keep them corraled, cool, and moist. They need not be kept in water.

Dropping a live crab in boiling water is needlessly cruel and thoroughly disconcerting as they often squeal. Better to kill a crab instantly by laying it on its back and splitting it down the middle with hatchet or knife. Lay the blade against the crab and give the cutting tool a sharp whack with a club—enough to cut through to the carapace (the hard shell over the back).

Holding the cutting tool in place, grasp one set of legs and pull, twisting to remove half the body meat along with the attached legs. Repeat on the other side. Rinse off any clinging innards or fragments of shell. Cook fifteen minutes in boiling sea water, then plunge the crab into cool water to soak for a few minutes, thereby making the meat much easier to remove from the shell.

**Shrimp.** Coon stripe shrimp (four to five inches long and found all along the West Coast from California to Alaska) are fun to catch when they migrate into shallow water in late summer and fall. At other times of year, they live one hundred to three hundred feet down on sand or gravel bottoms. Pulling a prawn trap from that depth is not easy in a kayak. But from August through November the big, tasty shrimp come within easy reach. Starting at dusk, you can catch them by lowering a baited trap from a dock. A trap can be a simple frame about four feet across with netting forming a shallow basket. Tie bait (such as a fish carcass) in the middle of the net. Pull the trap every fifteen minutes or so. As an alternative, walk (wearing knee boots or waders) or paddle along a protected shoreline with a flashlight and a kitchen strainer, colander, or dip net. The shrimps' eyes brightly reflect the flashlight's beam. Just scoop them up.

Keep shrimp alive in sea water. When ready to eat, pour that water out and dump the live shrimp into boiling sea water (they die instantly, unlike the larger crabs). Cook two to three minutes, until they turn pink. Plunge into cold water to cool; then peel.

## Bivalves

All bivalves—two-shelled mollusks including clams, oysters, mussels, and others—feed by filtering plankton from surrounding waters. During warm weather, when the water "blooms" with plankton (as in the phenomenon known as "red tide"), some of the plankton are poisonous. They do not harm the bivalves that feed on them, but the bivalves filter out and concentrate the toxins, becoming potentially poisonous. The toxins may remain in potentially harmful concentrations for a matter of days—or years! There is no known antidote. The result of eating poisonous shellfish can be serious illness or even death.

Do not harvest and eat bivalves of any kind without first checking with local authorities to assure there is no danger of Paralytic Shellfish Poisoning, commonly known as PSP.

**Clams.** The small, tasty bivalves, known collectively as "steamer clams," live beneath the sand or gravel of sheltered bays and inlets. Most are found within eighteen inches of the surface in the intertidal zone. The closer to the low-tide line, the richer and more sheltered the habitat. Dig straight down with hands or a simple tool. Or, on a rocky beach, "muddle" for clams by digging a hole and washing the sea water at its bottom against the sides.

Soak clams in sea water for four to eight hours (which may be accomplished by hanging them over the side of the kayak in a mesh bag). During this time, they clean themselves internally. Want stuffed clams? Scatter oatmeal or cornmeal on the surface of the water; the clams will feed on it. (Note that this is cornMEAL, not cornSTARCH, as I once inadvertently used, thereby creating something resembling cement-filled clams.)

Scrub clam shells and steam in one inch of water in a single layer in a covered frying pan about five minutes, until shells pop open. Discard any unopened clams.

**Oysters.** Not buried, but right on the bottom of warm-water bays and inlets, quiet bays and backwaters, live the oyster colonies. Look for them in the intertidal zone, where the larger ones are farther out. Although they may be harvested at any time of year, oysters are larger, firmer, and more flavorful from early winter until mid-May. After that, their energy goes into spawning, which leaves them depleted and less meaty.

Check local regulations before harvesting, as there are limits in most places. Gather in a mesh bag or pot; they need not be kept in water.

A favorite way of cooking fresh oysters is to barbecue them in the shell. After rinsing the oyster, lay it on a grill with the more rounded side of the shell on the bottom. Heat over coals until the shell opens slightly. Pry open the rest of the way with a fork, remove meat, dip in melted butter, and eat.

To shuck an oyster, insert a sharp knife between the shells and sever the adductor muscle. Place the oyster on a solid surface with the rounded side down. Insert the tip of the knife about halfway along an edge (not at the hinge), breaking off a bit of shell if necessary. Twist the knife and push in the blade, levering the handle upward and pushing the knife point down. When the muscle is severed, the shell will open easily, allowing you to scrape out all of the meat.

**Mussels.** Mussels of several kinds are found all along the coast, clinging to rocks, pilings, and floats in quiet waters. Paddle up to them and break them off by hand. Store out of the water, but keep cool and damp with seaweed or in a burlap sack. Scrub the shells well, pulling off the "beard." Steam twenty minutes, until shells pop open. (Mussels have the same seasonal cycle as oysters, at their peak for eating between early winter and mid-May.)

## Less Familiar Foods

**Limpets.** The little "Chinaman's hat" that measures up to an inch in diameter clings to the rocks on beaches all over the world. This single-shelled mollusk (like its cousin, the abalone) is one of the safest shellfish to harvest and eat. It lives on algae and does not feed on plankton as bivalves do, so it is not a potential carrier of PSP. And because it is so common, the "poor man's escargot" is valuable as emergency survival food.

Small limpets are found in the intertidal zone with the larger keyhole limpet (which has a hole in the peak) farther toward the ocean than the rest. Limpets cling to the rocks with a "foot" much like that of a snail; when alerted to possible danger, they cling tight. To gather them, move quietly and carry a knife to slip under the foot and pry up.

Leave limpets in sea water at least thirty minutes to clean themselves. Steam like clams in a single layer in a frying pan (they take five minutes to cook) or give the shells a scrub and drop the whole limpets into chowder for the last five minutes of cooking time. They also can be barbecued (see "Recipes").

**Abalone.** Larger than limpets are abalone, which may measure up to one foot wide. The larger species are found in the warmer waters of Mexico and California. Most common along the Northwest coast is the pinto abalone, usually three to four inches wide.

To gather abalone without diving, paddle along rocky shorelines in regions with plenty of tidal action. Look for patches of seaweed, on which abalone also feed. The best "ab" hunting by kayak is at the time of the lowest daylight tides in May, June, and July.

Abalone are well camouflaged. Their checkered mantles help you spot them (as do the white-specked edges). Move quietly and try not to let your shadow fall on the rocks. With stealth and a deft hand, you can grab the shell and remove it with a quick twist before the abalone grabs tight to the rock. A knife or spatula is essential to removing one that has clamped down.

Leave the abalone in sea water for thirty minutes before cutting the meat from the shell. Only the meat of the big abalone must be pounded to tenderize. Cut it crosswise and sauté until it is no longer translucent—only a few minutes. The meat also can be cut into bite-size pieces for chowder. Be careful not to overcook, as the meat then will become tough and rubbery.

**Sea urchins.** Looking more like underwater flowers than animals are the spiny sea urchins found on rocks just below low tide. Gather them by hand. The bright yellow ones are tastiest.

Open the bottom by cutting a circle around the center with a sharp knife. Pull out and discard the round, hard "Aristotle's lantern" from inside. Rinse and shake out all of the urchin's "insides," leaving only the light brown roe clinging to the shell. The roe—eggs—is what you eat: raw (sometimes mixed with soy sauce) on crackers or as dip, deep-fried in tempura batter, or beaten with eggs for an omelet from a true "chicken of the sea."

**Sea cucumber.** Not a vegetable, but a sea animal that resembles a cucumber in shape, this odd-looking creatures does you the favor of cleaning itself. When frightened it disgorges its inner organs as a defensive and diversionary tactic. The muscular outer cylinder can grow a new set of insides. Unfortunately for it, the muscle is the part you want to keep. Cut off the ends and then slice the tube lengthwise. Open it and you will see five longitudinal muscles. Pull each of them off in a whole chunk. Sauté or cut up for chowder. Cooking time is about five minutes.

# Beach Greens

**Seaweed.** Sea lettuce (*Ulva lactuca*) looks just like green, leafy lettuce growing about halfway up the tidal zone. It tastes like salty lettuce. Bladder wrack (*Fucus furcatus*) is a greenish brown rockweed, its forked branches tipped with yellow pods that pop when you step on them. (The pods are filled with a gelatinous substance used to thicken puddings, but that is not what you are interested in.) Cut off the topmost two or three inches where the pods have not yet puffed up. Use sea lettuce and "popweed" both as flavorings for soups and stews and as salad greens.

**Glasswort.** Called by many names including seabeach sandwort, chicken claws, crowfoot greens, and sea chickweed, this bright green plant with fleshy, succulent leaves grows just above the high-tide mark in sheltered inlets and bays. It sprawls over the sand, putting down roots as it grows. Eat the leaves raw in salads or cook the whole stem two minutes in salted water. Butter it and eat with your fingers, discarding the tough inner stem.

**Goosetongue.** Also called seashore plantain, this plant grows on rocky outcroppings near the water or well back on the beach. A cluster of leaves rises from the base of the plant, which also has a central stem with a spike of densely clustered greenish white flowers. Picking is best in early summer, when the tender new leaves are good to eat raw in salads. Boil or steam the larger leaves as cooked vegetables or use them to make wilted "lettuce" salad with bacon and vinegar.

# Berries

**Beach strawberries.** All along the West Coast from California to Alaska, wild strawberries are found in sunny spots at the top of the beach. They look just like the garden plants except smaller and closer to the ground. The leaves consist of three leaflets with toothed edges and the flower has five white petals. The bright red fruit is a real treat. You also can make tea from strawberry leaves. Boil about two handfuls of washed leaves in a quart of water for five minutes. Both the berries and leaves are rich in vitamin C.

**Blueberries.** Several subspecies grow along the West Coast, ranging from tall shrubs to little ones no more than two feet high. They grow in dappled sunlight as part of the forest understory, often right where the woods meet the beach. Some ripen as early as June and others as late as August and September. In Southeast Alaska the late-season berries often come complete with resident worms—tiny green things that look like baby inchworms. Many locals eat the berries worms and all. But if you would prefer to have berries alone, soak them for thirty minutes in fresh water with a few blueberry leaves floating on the surface. The worms will bail out and board the leaves as if they were life rafts. Discard leaves; eat berries. (Most authorities say to use sea water for this, but every worm I have encountered has headed for the lifeboats much more energetically in fresh water, leaving fewer casualties among the berries.)

**Salmonberries.** Growing on woody shrubs up to seven feet high, these look like big raspberries. It is common to find the full range of colors from pale pinkish yellow to bright red on the same bush. There may or may not be prickles on the twigs. Pick only those berries ripe enough to slip off easily. Compared to raspberries, salmonberries are somewhat bland. Add them to bowls of mixed berries, stir into compotes, or use in place of blueberries in muffins and pancakes.

# Food
# to
# Paddle
# On

Nobody ever died of scurvy because they forgot to pack the Tang for an overnight kayak trip. But plenty of paddlers on longer trips have become crabby or tired, and never connected the way they felt with what they ate.

On an extended kayak trip you are living in a nutritional world of your own making. It is unlikely you will be able to lay your hands on a food for which you develop a craving—perhaps nature's way of calling for something your body needs. It takes a little thinking ahead to make sure you have the right combination of foods to keep energy level and spirits high.

When I started paddling with Randel Washburne several years ago, he was intrigued with the things I brought to eat. It was not so much that they tasted good—he cooks and eats very well on the extended solo trips that are his specialty—but that I routinely used food to do something more than just satisfy a hearty appetite. Shivering in our sleeping bags one March night (when we would awake to find Barkley Sound a fantasy of frost), I shoved a candy bar in my mouth and handed him one to fire up the internal furnace, raising body heat. When we hit the beach tired and irritable after a long day of slogging into a southerly drizzle, I dug out a couple of granola bars to eat before we started to set up camp and collect firewood. Twenty minutes later we were starting to revive as blood sugar levels rose. An hour later we were still going strong because of the protein and carbohydrates we had taken in.

"That's fascinating," Randy said, as he started picking up on these nutritional tricks. "Why don't you tell people about these things?"

"Because most of them think nutrition is boring," I replied, recalling home ec classrooms of impatient teenagers tolerating the mandatory lecture before getting on with the interesting part of stirring up something to eat.

But at his urging, I now teach a seminar called "Food to Paddle On"—the basis for this chapter. The emphasis is not on diet and nutrition per se, but on how to put together a collection of food that adds up to something—a feeling of well-being backed up with reserves of stamina and energy. Provisions profoundly affect your spirits and performance. They are just as important as any other component of your gear.

## Water

So vital is water to the human body that two to three days without it can be fatal. The experts say it takes two to three quarts a day just to keep a body functioning. About half of that is supplied by the food we eat. The rest we drink in response to thirst, usually a good indicator of how much water we need to drink to top off the body's tank. Make sure you have plenty of fresh drinking water near at hand, and drink whenever you feel so inclined. In hot weather or when very active, you will want more—as you already know. Eating more concentrated and more dried foods, as is typical outdoors, also is likely to increase thirst. Kayakers in Baja, where weather is warm and water can be hard to find, figure on at least a half gallon of drinking water per person per day and carry more to allow for cooking.

You may have to remind yourself to drink enough water when you are cold. A cup of hot soup will sound much more appealing, but until you can wrap your hands around it do not neglect the water bottle.

## Covering All the Bases

The best diet is one that offers lots of variety. Because each food packs a different combination of nutrients, you increase the odds of getting everything you need by eating an assortment each day and by varying the assortment from one day to the next. People who try to simplify provisioning by packing large quantities of just a few things run the risk of short-changing themselves, as almost any prolonged limitation affects health. The flip side is that relying on a limited range of foods can result in an unhealthy overdose of elements that do not cause harm consumed in normal quantities. (Think of "coffee nerves" as an example.)

Ever since grade school, we have been taught about the "Four Basic Food Groups" and seen circle graphs with pictures of milk bottles and cheese in the upper left quadrant, carrots and apples in the next, etc. A good diet includes foods from each of the four groups each day. Here is a quick review with an eye toward paddling.

## Vegetables and Fruits

Each day's eating should include four servings. A single serving is one-half cup fresh fruit, vegetable, or juice. And those should be four different items, not one carrot and a cup and a half of applesauce. You can eat more; the four target servings are the minimum. One of them should be a food rich in vitamin C, which the body cannot store and needs to be given each day. Good sources of vitamin C are citrus fruits (oranges, grapefruit, lemons, tangerines), tomatoes, and dark green vegetables (spinach, green peppers, broccoli, parsley).

I usually mix up a quart of fruit juice, adding fresh water to powdered concentrate, to serve with breakfast and carry in addition to water for drinking during the day. If we do not have juice for breakfast, I often mix a quart of lemonade for citrus' sake. Dried fruit and fruit leathers are staples of lunch-sack fare. A big pot of fruit compote, a fruit cobbler, or warm applesauce with cinnamon or gingersnaps are desserts nobody is likely to refuse, and a great way of getting in the full complement of fruit. Fresh berries picked along the way and fresh fruits bought in town add variety. (Oranges and grapefruit travel beautifully in the bilge.)

Vegetables usually are harder than fruits to work into a traveling diet. I carry dehydrated ones and throw handfuls into almost any one-pot meal. A simple can of chili and beans gets doctored up with plenty of onion flakes, parsley and spinach flakes—maybe even some home-dried zucchini and a few dried tomatoes—and ends up tasting all the better for it. Good travelers include fresh carrots and cabbage and, to a lesser degree, celery, green peppers, and onions. Think of what lasts forever in the crisper drawer of your refrigerator; that's the stuff to pack. Grow alfalfa sprouts to sprinkle on stews and pile on sandwiches.

# Breads and Cereals

The minimum is four servings of four different things. Each serving is the equivalent of one slice of bread or a generous half-cup (somewhere between the one-half and three-quarters marks) of cooked cereal, cornmeal, or pasta. (At home, it also could be one cup of ready-to-eat cereal; Grapenuts is the only one of these that seems to go kayaking with any degree of frequency.) Each day include some whole-grain products to get the fiber, vitamins, and minerals lost when whole grains are milled. (Fiber, which is not broken down by the digestive system, plays an important role in preventing constipation; that can be a problem if paddlers spend long hours in their boats day after day.)

Hot cereal for breakfast is a favorite of ours. So are grilled English muffins and sourdough pancakes. Lunches often include pita bread, granola bars, and/or fig bars (the sturdy, flavorful kind made with whole wheat). And speaking of granola, with which so many people travel, remember that a handful of it may be half raisins, nuts, and sunflower seeds—good foods all, but they do not belong to the Breads and Cereals group, where it is easy to inadvertently count them when thinking back over what you have been eating that day. Dinner is an easy meal for getting in plenty of grain through rice and pasta and cornmeal. Matter of fact, most of us have a tendency to consume a disproportionate amount of breads and cereals late in the day. These foods are rich in carbohydrates, which sustain energy for many hours of activity. It is smarter to start the day with a good load of carbohydrates and to maintain that level with periodic refueling. The time you least need them for energy usually is just before hitting the sleeping bag.

# Milk and Cheese

Two servings a day is the target for these dairy products, important sources of calcium, protein, and vitamin D. Yogurt also belongs to this group, and is one of the things many paddlers crave (as are fresh milk and ice cream). A serving is one cup of milk or yogurt, or one and one-third ounces of cheese (about as much as in one of those thin, square slices they put on top of a burger in a fast-food restaurant). Cheese is easy to work into the menu, as so many hard cheeses travel well and are popular for lunch and snacking. Dry cheeses like Parmesan can be used to top one-pot dinners. Milk is harder to work in. I add instant dry milk powder to everything I bake and stir it into hot cereal. (Four tablespoons of powder gives you the same nutrients as a cup of milk.) And when I realize we have been skimping on the milk, I make pudding or cheesecake for dessert.

## Meat, Poultry, Fish, and Beans

Most Americans (indeed, most people who live in industrialized nations) eat more than they need from this high-protein category. All that nutrition requires is two servings a day. A serving is just two to three ounces of meat, poultry, or fish. (To visualize, consider that a Quarter Pounder by definition includes four ounces of meat.) It takes a larger amount of beans to make a serving, one to two cups of them. Other sources include eggs (one serving equals two eggs), peanut butter (four tablespoons per serving), and nuts or seeds (one-half to one cup per serving).

When kayakers express concern about keeping food from spoiling on an extended trip, most of the time they are visualizing one-pound packages of ground beef, T-bone steaks, and supermarket packages of fryer parts. These are, indeed, difficult to carry safely for any longer than a day. There is no reason not to eat them on the first day. But there is no need to carry large quantities of expensive freeze-dried meats to use later on. Smoking and marinating and spicing are age-old preservative treatments that make good traveling companions of meat—jerky, salami, pepperoni, and the like. A can of tuna contains between six and one-half and seven ounces, drained. That is more than enough fish to meet one person's need. Dry beans are easy to carry indefinitely and can be made into wonderful, hearty camp meals. Peanut butter is an excellent traveler, popular for both breakfast and lunch. A hearty breakfast omelet or dinner frittata makes a meal of eggs, either powdered or fresh. The sea and shore abound with fish and shellfish. Rarely does a kayaker have trouble getting enough of the food in this fourth group.

## Daily Menu

Eating the minimum amounts in all four groups gives you the basics, the full spectrum of nutrients. But it only adds up to about twelve hundred calories a day. That is not going to be enough to fuel an active adult, who can expect to burn between two thousand and four thousand calories a day on a kayak trip. Raise the number of calories by increasing the size of portions to satisfy your appetite (likely to be greater than usual because of increased physical activity). Also add some tasty fats and sweets.

The body uses fat for insulation, lubrication, and to store reserves of energy. At home, most people get plenty without thinking about it. There is fat in many of the foods from the Basic Four groups, and spreading a couple of teaspoonful of butter on toast or making a tuna sandwich with mayonnaise usually gives a body all it needs. Dried foods have less fat than their everyday counterparts, so kayakers (like backpackers) using many of them may find themselves craving more fatty things than usual. Peanut butter, nuts, and chocolate are easy and appealing answers. Fried and deep-fried foods help, too.

Here is an example of a day's menu covering the nutritional basics outlined above and well-suited to a kayak trip.

**Breakfast:**
1 fresh orange or tangerine
1 cup hot whole grain cereal
2 tablespoons milk powder stirred into cereal

**Lunch:**
1½ ounces Cheddar cheese
3 crackers
2 ounces salami
1 piece fruit leather
1 fresh carrot

**Dinner:**
4 ounces fresh-caught rockfish, steamed in foil with
1 cup vegetables (fresh onion, dried mushrooms, parsley, green
    pepper, and tomatoes)
¼ cup sour cream sauce (made from packaged mix and containing 2
    tablespoons dried milk powder
½ cup long grain and wild rice

Of course you are going to want to eat larger portions, not to mention snacks! The menu shows the minimum it would take to get the full range of foods from the Basic Four groups.

# Preventing "Energy Crash"

The English knew what they were doing when they instituted the tradition of afternoon tea. The feeling of burnout that often occurs in mid- to late afternoon is the body's way of letting you know it needs fuel. The quickest way to provide a quick pickup is with a bit of sugar (whether it be the sucrose of table sugar in a candy bar, the glucose of honey in granola, or the fructose in a piece of fruit). Tests have shown that blood sugar level rises within twenty minutes of eating simple carbohydrates (sugar). Unfortunately, those same tests show that after a little more than an hour it crashes to a lower level than before. The solution to the post-sugar crash is to eat some protein and complex carbohydrates (starches) along with the sugary snack. These slower-burning nutrients sustain the energy level far beyond the sugar "flash."

The munching that seems to begin in midmorning and continue through a couple of rounds of lunch typically tapers off by midafternoon, leaving kayakers vulnerable to a sag in energy about the time they have chosen a campsite but have a good hour or more before dinner is ready. To the rescue comes "tea time" or "cocktail hour"—call it what you may. The essential ingredients are a bite of something sweet and a bit of sturdier fare. A handful of granola or gorp will do the job in a pinch. However, many paddlers enjoy the ritual of a snack break featuring some treat that has not been wandering in and out of the lunch sack all day. (A cup of instant soup is wonderfully welcome on a cold or rainy day.) Thus fortified, energy and spirits rise and campers are not too ravenous to enjoy fixing dinner and eating sociably.

## Complementary Proteins

Anyone with passing familiarity with vegetarian eating has heard that the nutritional value of certain foods is enhanced by eating them along with certain others. The classic example is the combination of grains and legumes (beans). Almost every culture combines the two in at least one dish. Common in the culinary smorgasbord of the United States are peanut butter sandwiches, tortillas with refried beans, Boston baked beans with brown bread, the frontier staple of sourdough biscuits and beans, and rice with tofu, to name a few.

Meat and dairy products provide human bodies with "complete" protein, meaning that it closely resembles their own proportionate balance of the various amino acids of which protein is made. By contrast, protein from vegetable sources (such as nuts and beans) is low in one or two essential amino acids. The most efficient way to get the full complement of amino acids from vegetable sources is to eat more than one. Legumes (including beans, peas, and lentils) and grains (including wheat, rice, corn, and others) are complementary, together providing the full range of amino acids in proportions needed for human nutrition.

This is useful information for long kayak trips, for beans and grains are easily carried without refrigeration and may be combined in many appetizing ways. It is possible to achieve good nutrition with very small amounts of the meats, poultry, and fish which figure so prominently in everyday American eating.

Also applicable to all kayakers is the knowledge that eating legumes and grains in the same meal enhances their nutritional value; the whole is greater than the sum of its parts. When making a meal of chili beans, crumble the remains of the corn chips on top and you get more from the same two foods than when eating them at different times. Why not get the most "food value" out of the provisions you pack?

## Want to Know More?

The general information in this chapter is based on the nutritional needs of healthy adults. Children, teenagers, pregnant women, and people taking certain types of medication are among those who have additional or special needs. It is beyond the scope of this book to offer complete information on diet and nutrition. But if what you have read here piques your interest, there are several excellent, readable sources of further information (including more complete explanations of protein complementarity) listed in the back of this book.

# Menu Planning

Menu planning begins with what you like to eat. For me, that usually includes looking through recipes and lists of provisions from previous trips. This is a project tailor-made for brightening a gloomy off-season day when you can fiddle with food-planning at leisure and experiment with unfamiliar recipes.

For super-convenience, copy recipes in this book and any others that lend themselves to kayak cookery onto four-by-six-inch index cards, putting the list of ingredients on the front and the directions on the back. That should leave plenty of room for notes about tailoring to your personal taste, cooking equipment, and the like. When planning menus, sort through the cards and select those with greatest appeal.

Next, sort them into two piles, those requiring fresh ingredients and those that do not. In making your final choices, choose from both groups. In deciding how much fresh food to carry, you may wish to refer to the chart showing how long certain foods last (in "Fresh Starts") and general guidelines (in "Provisioning for a Long Trip").

Then comes the fun of building menus day by day, deciding what combination of foods appeals to your palate. You may wish to check the results against the nutritional guidelines in "Food to Paddle On."

No need to make an extensive grocery list; just take your chosen recipe cards when you go grocery shopping. In using recipes or packaged mixes designed for home use rather than as camping fare, mentally cut in half the estimated number of servings to allow for the hearty appetites and simpler menus typical of outdoor life.

Another factor that may need adjusting is preparation time. Slicing vegetables for stir-frying may take just ten minutes with the food processor on the kitchen counter, but a half hour with a Swiss army knife on a drift log. On each recipe in this book we have estimated campsite preparation time. That certainly affects what I prepare on a given day! You may wish to estimate in-camp preparation time for other recipes as you add them to your file and repertoire.

And whenever you forget to pack a key ingredient, make a disaster of cooking, or fix something new that nobody wants to eat a second time, be assured that all of us who have been doing this sort of thing for any length of time have been in the same boat. Start with what you like and what strikes you as manageable. Your skills in kayak cookery will grow as surely as your boat-handling and sea sense. Enjoy them all!

# Sample Menus

Capitalized recipes appear in this book. (See Index for page numbers).

SATURDAY

**Breakfast:**
Your choice, eaten at home or restaurant on the way to the put-in point.

**Lunch:**
A picnic at the put-in point before launching. Make your own sandwiches with Kaiser rolls, cream cheese, sliced ham, fresh tomato, avocado, and sprouts.
individual bottles of fruit juice (assorted)
Chocolate Chip Bars

**Snack:**
instant tomato soup

**Dinner:**
barbecued chicken (frozen, split broilers and marinade brought from home)
Roast Corn on the Cob
tossed green salad
sourdough bread with butter

SUNDAY

**Breakfast:**
fresh orange juice (bought in a cardboard carton)
Mexican Eggs
hash brown potatoes
coffee

**Lunch:**
tuna sandwiches with sprouts and tomatoes in pita (pocket) bread
fresh plums and nectarines

**Snack:**
last of the Chocolate Chip Bars

**Dinner:**
Stir-fry Supper
steamed rice
vanilla pudding splashed with sherry (optional)

MONDAY

**Breakfast:**
Granola with yogurt and fresh fruit (remaining plums and nectarines)
coffee

**Lunch:**
celery and carrot sticks
bagels with cream cheese and smoked salmon

**Snack:**
crackers with Swiss cheese

**Dinner:**
fresh asparagus
Foil-roasted Salmon
Roasted Potatoes with Onions
imported, filled chocolate bars

TUESDAY

**Breakfast:**
fresh cantaloupe
Crab Omelet
coffee

**Lunch:**
Peanut Butter and What?
chunks of semisweet chocolate

**Snack:**
Egg Drop Soup

**Dinner:**
Fresh Artichokes
Mac and Cheese Deluxe
hot applesauce with ginger snaps

WEDNESDAY

**Breakfast:**
fresh grapefruit
corned beef hash (canned or home-dried)
grilled sourdough English muffins
coffee

**Lunch:**
fig bars with peanut butter
tangerines
carrot sticks

**Snack:**
Hummus Dip with olives

**Dinner:**
Fish and Chips (made with fresh-caught rockfish), served with lemon and
    vinegar.
Coleslaw
hot chocolate with instant dry milk powder and brandy (optional)

THURSDAY

**Breakfast:**
grape drink (fortified with vitamin C)
hot kipper snacks on English muffins

**Lunch:**
sharp Cheddar cheese, tart apples, and crackers
assorted candy bars

**Snack:**
miso soup with extra dry vegetable flakes

**Dinner:**
Rice Curry
Mystery Pudding

FRIDAY

**Breakfast:**
Old-Fashioned Sourdough Pancakes with fresh-picked blueberries
Maple Syrup

**Lunch:**
pepperoni
granola bars
dried apricots and prunes

**Snack:**
Swiss cheese and crackers

**Dinner:**
Judy's Creative Bouillabaisse (with fresh ingredients)
cornbread
cheesecake (made from packaged mix)

SATURDAY

**Breakfast:**
hot cereal (with instant dry milk powder added) and maple sugar crystals

**Lunch:**
lemonade
smoky Cheddar cheese spread and crackers
assorted fruit leathers
fresh almonds

**Snack:**
tortilla chips with salsa

**Dinner:**
Tamale Pie (made with TVP or home-dried ground beef)
Swedish Fruit Soup

SUNDAY

**Breakfast** (quick-start morning to catch the tide for return trip home):
orange juice (made from powder the previous night)
freeze-dried roast beef hash with potatoes
instant coffee

**Lunch** (at take-out point):
cheeseburger with the works
fresh milk

**Snack** (after unloading boats and gear):
corn chips and beer

**Dinner:**
your choice, at home or restaurant

# PART TWO

### Recipes

# Make It
# and
# Take It

# Granola

**Yield:** 5 cups
**Preparation time at home:** 1 hour

*Here is one homemade version of the ever-popular, hearty cereal-plus-nuts.*

2½ cups rolled oats
½ cup wheat germ
½ cup flaked coconut (unsweetened)
½ cup finely chopped raw cashews
½ cup finely chopped pecans
½ cup raw sunflower seeds
⅛ cup water
⅛ cup oil
2 tablespoons honey
2 tablespoons molasses
1 teaspoon vanilla
½ teaspoon cinnamon
1 cup raisins

**At home:** Stir together oats, wheat germ, coconut, cashews, pecans, and sunflower seeds. In small saucepan, combine all liquid ingredients and cinnamon. Stirring, heat just to boiling point. Quickly pour over dry ingredients and mix thoroughly. Spread on cookie sheet and bake 30 minutes at 325°, stirring occasionally to dry evenly. Cool. Stir in raisins. Bag airtight.

**In camp:** Serve with milk as breakfast cereal. Stir into yogurt and dip up with fresh apple slices. Sprinkle on top of warm pudding or fruit compote.

## Randy's Beef Jerky Marinade

**Yield:** Enough to marinate 1 pound meat
**Preparation time at home:** 5 minutes

*Our favorite marinade recipe is this one, which has evolved by experiment and accident. To make beef jerky, see the "Food Drying" chapter.*

1 tablespoon brown sugar
½ teaspoon garlic powder
¼ teaspoon black pepper
1 tablespoon low-sodium soy sauce
2 tablespoons Worcestershire sauce
1 tablespoon bottled steak sauce
1 tablespoon ketchup

**At home:** Mix all ingredients in a jar and shake well.

## Beef Jerky Marinade: Barbecue Flavor

**Yield:** Enough to marinate 1 pound meat
**Preparation time at home:** 5 minutes

*It is said that you should never cook with wine that you would not like to drink. Likewise, do not make a marinade for jerky with a barbecue sauce you would not enjoy in a barbecued beef sandwich. Upon discovering a restaurant that made the best barbecue sauce I ever ate, I bought a pint of it to take home for making jerky—a great success! To make beef jerky, see the "Food Drying" chapter.*

4 tablespoons bottled barbecue sauce
2 tablespoons red wine vinegar or cider vinegar
¼ teaspoon black pepper

**At home:** Mix all ingredients in a jar and shake well.

# Beef Jerky Marinade: Burgundy Flavor

**Yield:** Enough to marinate 1 pound meat
**Preparation time at home:** 5 minutes

*Do not judge the success of this recipe on the basis of jerky that has just been dried. The flavor develops with a few days' storage. To make beef jerky, see the "Food Drying" chapter.*

¼ cup burgundy or other full-flavored red wine
2 tablespoons tomato paste
½ teaspoon salt powder
½ teaspoon garlic powder
¼ teaspoon black pepper

**At home:** Mix all ingredients in a jar and shake well.

# Almost-Instant Brown Rice

**Yield:** 2 cups cooked rice
**Preparation time at home:** 2 hours

*If you like brown rice but shy away from it when camping because it takes so long to cook, here is help. You can cut the campsite cooking time to less than that of white rice by precooking at home. This technique works equally well with wild rice or with the popular combination of brown and wild rice.*

3½ cups water (divided)
1 cup brown rice

**At home:** Bring 1½ cups water to boil and stir in rice. Cover pot, reduce heat, and simmer about 45 minutes, until all water has been absorbed by rice. Spread on cookie sheet and bake 1 hour at 200°, stirring occasionally to dry evenly. Cool. Pack airtight in plastic bag.

**In camp:** Bring 2 cups water to boil and stir in rice. Cover and simmer about 10 minutes, until all water has been absorbed by rice.

# Poppy Seed Cake

**Yield:** 2 loaf cakes, 8 slices in each
**Preparation time at home:** 1 hour

*Easy to make, this moist cake keeps well if protected from crushing. (A single loaf fits into an empty coffee can.) Take one loaf kayaking and freeze the second loaf for your next trip.*

18 ounces (1 box) yellow cake mix
3 ounces (1 small box) butterscotch-flavored instant pudding mix
2 or more ounces (1 box) poppy seeds
4 eggs
½ cup oil
1 cup warm water

**At home:** Combine all ingredients in mixing bowl and beat 4 minutes. Pour into 2 greased loaf pans. Bake at 350° for 45 minutes, or until toothpick inserted in center of cake comes out clean. Cool about 10 minutes in pans before turning out to finish cooling on racks. (Cake fresh from the oven comes apart when it is turned out. If cooled completely in the pan, it may balk at coming out.) Wrap each loaf in foil or plastic bag and cut off 1-inch slices as desired.

**Variation:** Substitute lemon-flavored cake mix and lemon-flavored instant pudding mix.

# Russian Tea

**Yield:** 5½ cups tea mix (about 24 servings)
**Preparation time at home:** 5 minutes

*Here is a basic recipe for a popular, energy-boosting hot drink to brighten an overcast or rainy day. Vary the proportions of ingredients to custom-tailor your own special blend.*

2 ounces instant tea
1 packet unsweetened lemonade mix (enough to make 1 to 2 quarts lemonade)
17.6 ounces (1 jar) instant orange-flavor breakfast drink
1 cup sugar
2 teaspoons ground cinnamon
1 teaspoon ground cloves

**At home:** Measure and mix together all ingredients. Pack in an airtight, reclosable container.

**In camp:** Put three heaping tablespoons into cup, add boiling water, and stir.

## Cardamom Snack Bars

**Yield:** 16
**Preparation time at home:** 1 hour

*Marcia Herrin is the creator of this recipe, first published by the Good Food Store in Missoula, Montana. She says that cardamom tastes like "a cross between ginger and cinnamon with a little lemon and lime thrown in."*
2 cups whole wheat flour
1 tablespoon baking powder
¼ cup grated lemon peel
¼ cup grated orange peel
2 teaspoons cinnamon
½ teaspoon ground cardamom
¼ teaspoon ground cloves
½ cup sunflower seeds or walnuts
1 cup honey
3 tablespoons margarine

**At home:** In mixing bowl, combine all ingredients except honey and margarine. Set aside. Melt and stir together honey and margarine. Pour over dry ingredients and mix thoroughly. Pat into a greased 9-by-12-inch pan. Bake 20 to 25 minutes in oven preheated to 350°. Cool. Cut into bars about 2½ by 3 inches and wrap individually in plastic.

## Chocolate Chip Bars

**Yield:** 2 dozen
**Preparation time at home:** 1 hour

*Granola is great for snacking in camp, but when eating in the boat it is much easier to handle a mixture baked into a bar. Here is an exceptionally good recipe.*

¾ cup butter
½ cup brown sugar
½ cup honey
1 teaspoon vanilla
1 cup dried apricots, chopped
1 cup currants or raisins
1 cup flaked unsweetened coconut
½ cup coarsely chopped walnuts
1 cup slivered or sliced almonds
½ cup rolled oats
1 cup wheat germ
2 cups chocolate chips
1 egg

**At home:** In small saucepan, melt butter. Add brown sugar, honey, and vanilla, stirring well to blend. Set aside to cool while mixing dry ingredients.

In large bowl, combine all fruits, nuts, grain, and chocolate chips. In small bowl, beat egg. Stir it into butter mixture and, stirring, drizzle over dry ingredients. Mix thoroughly.

Pat into greased 9-by-13-inch cake pan. Bake at 325° for 45 minutes. Cool. Cut into 24 bars, each about 1½ by 3 inches. Wrap each one in plastic wrap.

# Breakfast Miscellany

## Skillet Hominy

**Serves:** 2
**Preparation time in camp:** 10 minutes

*How long has it been since you had hominy? Stir up this simple-but-satisfying skilletful for breakfast or as a side dish with fish.*

1 tablespoon oil
14½ ounces (1 can) hominy, drained
1 packet Butter Buds
4 to 8 ounces plain yogurt
Salt and cracked black pepper to taste

**In camp:** Heat oil in skillet. Sauté hominy, sprinkling Butter Buds over it as you do so. Stir in yogurt and heat, stirring. Serve with salt and cracked black pepper.

# Jiffy Cornbread Cakes

**Serves:** 2
**Preparation time in camp:** 15 minutes

*Served with hot maple syrup and sausage, this is one of my favorite hearty breakfasts. (Maple sugar granules [see Maple Syrup recipe] and home-dried sausages [see "Food Drying" chapter] make the whole meal compact and long-lasting.)*

1 package Jiffy Corn Muffin Mix
3 tablespoons instant dry milk powder
2½ tablespoons dried egg powder (optional)
¾ cup water
Margarine

**At home:** Stir together all dry ingredients and seal in zip locking bag.

**In camp:** In small bowl, stir water into dry ingredients, stirring just enough to blend. Batter will be slightly lumpy. Set aside to let the batter begin puffing up (about 5 minutes).

Meanwhile, melt about 1 tablespoon margarine in skillet. Drop batter from mixing spoon onto hot skillet, making 2 or 3 puddles, each about 2 inches in diameter. Fry about 2 minutes on each side, until golden brown. Repeat until batter is used up, adding margarine to skillet as needed. Serve with additional margarine, if desired.

**Note:** Directions on the corn muffin mix package call for adding 1 egg. If you have a fresh egg and want to use it, fine. But this is a case where you will not be able to tell the difference between powdered egg and fresh, and you do not really have to add any egg at all. Honest.

# Maple Syrup

**Serves:** 2
**Preparation time in camp:** A few minutes

*This is so simple (and so good!) that I will never mess with carrying syrup again.*

⅛ cup water
¼ cup maple sugar granules

**In camp:** Bring water to boil. Add maple sugar granules and stir until dissolved.

# Couscous with Fruit

**Serves:** 2
**Preparation time in camp:** 10 minutes

*Couscous is the fastest cooking of all the whole grains, matching the speed of breakfast cereals that have been processed to make them quick to fix. Bright gold in color, couscous is pretty, too.*

1 cup couscous
4 tablespoons instant dry milk powder
1 teaspoon cinnamon
¼ cup dried nectarines or apricots, cut in small pieces
¼ cup pitted prunes, cut in small pieces
¼ cup currants
¼ cup slivered almonds
3 cups water
More milk (optional)

**At home:** Mix and bag together the couscous, milk powder, and cinnamon. Separately mix and bag the fruits and nuts.

**In camp:** Bring water to boil. Stir in couscous mix and simmer 5 minutes. Stir in fruits and nuts. Cover and set aside to steam 5 minutes. Serve as is, or topped with more milk.

# French Toast

**Serves:** 2
**Preparation time in camp:** 15 minutes

*Here is a suitable send-off for French bread left over from the previous night's cheese fondue. Serve with sausage or bacon and hot maple syrup.*

4 tablespoons dried egg powder
3 tablespoons instant dry milk powder
Pinch salt
⅔ cup water
6 slices French bread

**In camp:** Combine egg powder, milk powder, and salt. Add water a little at a time, beating to prevent lumping. Dip bread into mixture and set aside to let liquid soak in.

Grill on lightly greased, hot skillet until golden brown on both sides. Serve with margarine and hot maple syrup.

**Note:** You may want to cut bread slices in half to fit better into skillet.

# Overnight Cereal

**Serves:** 1
**Preparation time in camp:** 5 minutes

*Just before hitting the sleeping bag, use the last of the hot water to fix breakfast while you sleep. This is a favorite ploy of paddlers who like to get onto the water early in the day.*

⅓ cup whole grain cereal
3 tablespoons instant dry milk powder
Pinch salt (optional)
⅔ cup boiling water
Maple sugar granules (optional)

**In camp:** Measure cereal, milk powder, and salt into wide-mouth thermos bottle. Pour in water, cap tightly, and swirl to blend contents. Set aside until morning. Uncap and pour out hot cereal, ready to eat. Sprinkle with maple sugar granules, if desired.

# Crab Benedict

**Serves:** 2
**Preparation time in camp:** 20 minutes

*Two cooks working side by side can turn out this elegant breakfast with ease, one grilling muffins while the other poaches eggs.*

Hollandaise sauce (made from packaged mix)
About ½ cup cooked crab meat
2 English muffins, split and buttered
4 fresh eggs

**In camp:** Prepare hollandaise sauce according to package directions. Gently stir in crab meat and set aside.

    Grill English muffins and poach eggs. Spoon sauce onto each muffin half, top with poached egg and additional sauce.

# Mexican Eggs

**Serves:** 2
**Preparation time in camp:** 10 minutes

*This eye-opening breakfast entrée is the invention of Carol and Jack Hilton of Seattle, Washington. Serve with hash brown potatoes made from a packaged dry mix.*

½ onion, chopped
2 tablespoons oil
4 ounces chopped green chilies
¼ cup bacon bits or diced cooked ham
1 tomato, diced
1 cup grated Cheddar cheese
6 eggs, beaten
Salt and pepper

**In camp:** Sauté onion in oil until golden. Stir in chilies, bacon bits, tomato, and cheese. Cook, stirring, until hot; push toward edges of pan. Pour eggs into center and stir slightly as they start cooking. Stir partly cooked eggs into rest of ingredients and continue cooking a minute or two until eggs have set. Season with salt and pepper.

# Chicken Hash

**Serves:** 2
**Preparation time in camp:** 15 minutes

*Roast an extra potato over an evening campfire to save for a hearty breakfast of Chicken Hash.*

1 medium onion, chopped
Oil
1 baked potato, diced
12 ounces (1 can) corn, drained
6 ounces (1 can) chicken, drained
1 large fresh tomato, diced
Pinch basil
Salt and cracked black pepper
Sour cream sauce (optional), made from packaged mix

**In camp:** Sauté onion in oil until translucent. Add potato, corn, chicken, tomato, and basil; sauté, turning occasionally, until hot. Serve with salt and pepper and topped with sour cream sauce.

**Note:** For a longer lasting meal package, use freeze-dried chicken chunks, home-dried or freeze-dried corn, and dried tomatoes. But for the sake of texture, use fresh onion and potato—both of which travel well.

# Scrambled Wheat

**Serves:** 2 or 3
**Preparation time at home:** A few minutes
**Preparation time in camp:** 15 minutes

*Bulgur, a cracked wheat cereal, joins vegetables in a hearty scrambled-egg dish that is equally good for breakfast or dinner.*

¼ cup bulgur cracked wheat
2 tablespoons dried onion flakes
2 tablespoons dried green pepper flakes
2 tablespoons dried tomato flakes
1 tablespoon dried parsley flakes
¾ cup dried egg powder
2 tablespoons instant dry milk powder
½ teaspoon marjoram
½ teaspoon oregano
½ teaspoon thyme
½ teaspoon salt
Dash pepper
¼ cup bacon bits, diced pepperoni, or hard salami (optional)
3½ cups water (divided)

**At home:** Mix and bag together the bulgur and dried vegetables. Mix and bag together the egg powder, milk powder, and seasonings. Package the bacon bits separately or, in camp, add pepperoni or salami from lunch provisions.

**In camp:** Bring 2 cups of the water to boil. Stir in bulgur mixture and simmer until most of water is absorbed. Add bacon bits, if desired.

Pour dried egg mixture into wide-mouth poly bottle and add 1½ cups water. Shake well to blend. Pour over bulgur mixture and scramble together over heat until eggs set to the degree of firmness you like.

# For Lunch and Late-day Snacks

# Peanut Butter and What?

**Serves:** 2
**Preparation time in camp:** A few minutes

*Peanut butter is a stalwart traveler, so much so that it gets boring over the long haul. For a change of pace, pack it in the lunch bag with an unexpected companion ingredient.*

2 English muffins
4 tablespoons peanut butter
6 dried pitted prunes
    or
1 banana, sliced
about ½ cup alfalfa sprouts
    or
2 tablespoons crumbled bacon bits

**In camp:** Split muffins and spread half of each with peanut butter. Top with either prunes, sliced banana and sprouts, or bacon bits. Cover with second half of muffin.

# Peanut Butter Spread

**Yield:** About 1½ cups
**Preparation time at home:** 10 minutes

*There are as many variations on Peanut Butter Spread as there are people who like it. This version is particularly good with Heavy Bread or English muffins with raisins.*

1 cup chunky peanut butter
½ cup instant dry milk powder
½ cup molasses
Honey to taste (optional)
1 tablespoon soft margarine

**At home:** Mix all ingredients and pack in a screw-top plastic container.

**Variation:** Make with smooth peanut butter and carry in a refillable plastic squeeze tube.

## Heavy Bread

**Yield:** 2 loaves
**Preparation time at home:** ½ hour to prepare, 1½ hours to bake

*Heavy Bread is solid and moist. The original recipe, from which this version was adapted, was developed for backpackers by Diana Reetz-Stacy and first published by the Good Food Store in Missoula, Montana. The sturdy, tasty bread soon proved equally popular with kayakers.*

2½ cups plain yogurt
3 or 4 mashed, ripe bananas
¼ cup oil
¼ cup honey
1 tablespoon salt
1 cup coarsely chopped walnuts
1 cup dried apricots, each half cut into quarters
1 cup raisins
9 to 10 cups whole wheat flour

**At home:** Mix together yogurt, bananas, oil, honey, and salt. Add walnuts, apricots, and raisins. Stir in flour 1 cup at a time. When dough holds together, knead until it becomes elastic. Shape into 2 loaves. Place on greased cookie sheet or in greased bread pans and bake 1¼ to 1½ hours at 350°. Cool completely before packing in plastic bag.

## Logan Bread

**Yield:** 2 loaves
**Preparation time at home:** 30 minutes to prepare, 3 hours to bake

*A backpacking staple, nutritious Logan Bread travels equally well in a kayak. Those who like to eat it with cheese at lunchtime usually omit the cinnamon and raisins. Raisins help keep it moist and give it more appeal to eat by itself as a snack. I like to make the simpler version, and after pouring half the dough into a loaf pan, add cinnamon and raisins to the dough for the second loaf. (If you follow suit, add half the amounts of cinnamon and raisins listed in the full recipe.)*

6 cups whole wheat flour
¾ cup brown sugar
¼ cup instant dry milk powder
½ teaspoon salt
1 teaspoon baking powder
½ teaspoon ground cinnamon (optional)
½ pound melted margarine
2 cups water
¾ cup honey
¾ cup molasses
½ cup chopped nuts
½ cup raisins (optional)

**At home:** In large mixing bowl, combine flour, brown sugar, milk powder, salt, baking powder, and cinnamon. To melted margarine, add water, honey, and molasses; mix well and pour over flour mixture, stirring to blend. Add nuts and raisins.

Pour batter into 4 greased loaf pans and bake 1½ hours at 350°. Cover with foil and bake 1½ hours longer. Turn out of pans to cool. Seal each loaf in plastic bag, or slice and wrap each piece in foil. It will keep at room temperature for at least 2 weeks.

# Grilled Cheese Sandwiches

**Serves: 2**
**Preparation time in camp:** 10 minutes

2 English muffins, split and spread with margarine
4 ounces cheese (any kind), sliced thin

**In camp:** In skillet, grill muffins split-side down until golden brown. Turn and lay cheese on grilled face. Cover pan to hold heat a few minutes as cheese melts and muffin bottoms brown.

**Variation:** Sprinkle precooked bacon bits or slivers of salami over hot muffins before adding cheese.

# Egg Drop Soup

**Serves:** 2
**Preparation time in camp:** 5 minutes

*This makes good use of an aging egg (or two) and green onion. Make it for a lunch to brighten a drizzly day in camp or as a spirit-and-energy reviving late-afternoon snack.*

2 cups water
2 bouillon cubes (vegetable or chicken)
1 or 2 eggs, beaten
1 green onion, finely chopped

**In camp:** Bring water to boil and stir in bouillon cubes, dissolving them. Then stir in beaten egg, muddling the broth a bit as the egg solidifies in strands. Pour into mugs and top each with a generous sprinkling of onion.

# Bagels with The Works

**Serves:** 2 for lunch, 4 for snacks
**Preparation time in camp:** A few minutes

*Especially appreciated as a snack at the end of a long day of paddling, these bagels are quick to fix with a minimum of messing around. Carry the cream cheese next to your boat's bottom to keep it cool. (Stir leftover cream cheese and/or salmon into an omelet for breakfast the next day.)*

4 to 6 bagels
3 ounces (1 package) cream cheese
3¼ ounces (1 can) smoked salmon

**In camp:** Split bagels. Spread with cream cheese and top with smoked salmon.

# Skillet Bean Dip

**Serves:** 2 generously
**Preparation time in camp:** 10 minutes

16 ounces (1 can) spicy refried beans with chopped green chilies
Sour cream sauce (made from packet of dry mix) or 1 cup plain yogurt
1 fresh tomato, diced
2 green onions, chopped
Tortilla chips for dipping

**In camp:** Heat refried beans in skillet. Remove from heat and quickly spread reconstituted sour cream sauce over top. Sprinkle with tomato and onion. Dip from skillet with tortilla chips.

**Variation:** Add a layer of Cheddar cheese, sprinkling about ½ cup cheese on top of hot beans in skillet and continuing to heat until cheese starts to melt. Then layer on toppings as above.

# Hummus Dip

**Serves:** 4
**Preparation time in camp:** 10 minutes

*Here is another palate-pleasing and nutritious solution to the late-afternoon energy slump. No reason why you cannot mix hummus and slice vegetables early in the day; keep cool until munch time.*

6 ounces (1 package) dry hummus-with-tahini mix
Water
4 carrots
4 stalks celery
6 ounces (1 can) pitted black olives

**In camp:** Mix hummus mix with water to reconstitute according to package directions (which vary slightly from brand to brand). Drain olives. Cut carrots and celery into 2-inch sticks.

Scoop up hummus with vegetables and olives. (A fork or toothpick helps in dipping the latter.)

# Popcorn

**Serves:** 4
**Preparation time in camp:** 5 to 10 minutes

2 tablespoons oil
⅛ cup popcorn
Seasoning: Butter Buds, salt, Parmesan cheese, herbs and spices

**In camp:** Tear heavy-duty foil into 4 squares, each as long as the roll of foil is wide. Divide oil and popcorn equally, placing ¼ of each in the center of each foil square. Bring up the corners to form a loose pouch, crimping edges so exploding kernels cannot escape.

Insert top of each foil pouch into a slit cut in the end of a 3-foot (or longer) stick. Crimp (or wire) pouch tightly to stick.

Holding other end of stick, place bottom of pouch on grill or directly on hot coals. Shake stick as corn pops. Open pouch and add seasoning.

# Fresh Seafood

## Foil-Roasted Salmon or Rockfish

**Serves:** 2 people per pound of fish
**Preparation time in camp:** 6 to 10 minutes per pound of fish

1 whole salmon or rockfish, cleaned with head and tail removed
Oil
Salt and pepper to taste
1 fresh lemon, thinly sliced
1 whole onion, thinly sliced

**In camp:** Rinse fish, brushing off any loose scales. Rub inside and out with oil. Sprinkle inside with salt and pepper. Lay fish on foil and place slices of lemon and onion in cavity and along sides. Fold edges of foil to seal package well, then wrap and seal in a second layer of foil. Place fish on rack over coals and cook, turning at least once. Fish is done when it flakes easily from bone at thick end. Serve with fresh lemon wedges.

# Rockfish en Reynolds

**Serves:** 4
**Preparation time in camp:** 45 minutes

*This meal-in-a-packet lends itself to embellishment. If the fillets are not very big, top them with canned shrimp (dividing one can among four packets). Or enclose spinach—dried, fresh, or frozen—placing it over the mushrooms.*

4 rockfish fillets
16 fresh mushrooms
1 package dry cream-of-leek soup mix
1 pint sour cream
Steamed brown rice (or long grain and wild rice) to serve 4

**In camp:** Lightly grease 4 squares of aluminum foil and place rockfish fillet in center of each. Slice 4 mushrooms onto each fillet. Stir together soup mix and sour cream; spoon over mushrooms. Wrap each serving in foil, folding and crimping edges so packet will not leak. Wrap in a second layer of foil. Cook on grill over coals 20 to 30 minutes, turning once. Serve on steamed brown rice.

**Variation:** For rockfish fillets, substitute two 6-ounce cans chicken or 1 package freeze-dried chicken chunks, reconstituted.

# Fish and Chips

**Serves:** 2
**Preparation time in camp:** 30 minutes

*With fresh-caught cod, this is ambrosia.*

6 ounces (1 package) Betty Crocker dry hash brown potatoes
Water
Oil
1 cup Peppy's Fish Batter mix
About ⅓ cup water
½ to 1 pound fresh fish fillets
Vinegar or lemon juice
Salt and pepper

**In camp:** Pour dry potatoes into skillet. Add water as needed to reconstitute as you simmer them, adding oil to brown. (See package directions for details.)

Meanwhile, heat oil for deep-frying. Mix Peppy's Fish Batter mix with enough water to make a medium-thick batter. Cut fish fillets into pieces about 2 inches square. Dip each piece of fish in batter to coat, shake off excess and deep-fry a few pieces at a time until batter is golden and fish is done. (Thin batter slightly, if needed to cook evenly.) Drain fish on paper towels and cover to keep warm. Serve heaped on hash browns. Sprinkle vinegar or lemon juice over everything; add salt and pepper to taste.

## Sweet and Sour Fish

**Serves:** 4
**Preparation time in camp:** 30 minutes

2 pounds rockfish fillets, cut in bite-size pieces
⅓ cup cornstarch
4 tablespoons oil (divided)
1 clove garlic, minced
1 medium onion, sliced and separated into rings
1 large green pepper, cut into 1-inch pieces
8 ounces (1 can) pineapple chunks
About 1 cup sweet and sour sauce (made from packaged mix)
Cooked rice

**In camp:** Shake fish in plastic bag with cornstarch to coat pieces. Brown in 2 tablespoons of the oil. Remove fish to drain on paper towels and cover to keep warm.

Add remaining oil to pan and sauté garlic, onion, and green pepper. Drain pineapple chunks, reserving liquid.

Prepare sweet and sour sauce according to package directions, using juice drained from pineapple, if desired. Pour into pan and cook, stirring, until sauce thickens. Stir in pineapple chunks and heat about 1 minute. Serve fish with cooked rice, spooning sauce on top.

# Seafood Sauté

**Serves:** 2
**Preparation time in camp:** 10 minutes

1 cup fresh mushrooms, sliced
4 tablespoons butter, melted
8 ounces fresh rockfish fillets, scallops, oysters, or combination thereof
¼ cup white wine
1 tablespoon dried parsley flakes (optional)
Lemon wedges

**In camp:** Sauté mushrooms in butter until golden. Add fish and sauté on both sides. Add wine (and parsley, if desired), cover, and steam 1 minute. Remove cover and continue cooking until done. Serve with lemon wedges.

# Grilled Oysters

**Serves:** 2
**Preparation time in camp:** 20 minutes

1 packet Butter Buds
½ cup dry bread crumbs with Italian seasoning
1 pint (about 8) fresh oysters
1 egg, beaten
Salt and pepper
Lemon wedges

**In camp:** Mix Butter Buds with bread crumbs. Shuck oysters. Dip in beaten egg and coat with crumb mixture. Fry in oil until golden brown, about 3 minutes on each side. Serve hot with salt, pepper, and lemon wedges.

# Gingered Clams

**Serves:** 2
**Preparation time in camp:** 10 minutes

*This fresh approach to simple steamed clams came from Pansy Bray of
Hoquiam, Washington.*

1 pound steamer clams
4 tablespoons toasted sesame oil
3 slices fresh ginger, minced
2 tablespoons soy sauce

**In camp:** Scrub clams and drain. Heat oil in deep skillet or wok and
stir-fry ginger 30 seconds. Stir in soy sauce and clams. Cook, stirring,
until all clams pop open. Sea water from their shells mingles with the
seasonings to make a flavorful broth. Dip the meat into it, then drink
what is left.

# Grilled Limpets

**Serves:** 2
**Preparation time in camp:** About 10 minutes

12 to 18 large limpets
Lemon juice
   or
Melted butter with garlic powder

**In camp:** Rinse limpets in sea water. Place shell-side down on grill
over hot coals. Cook until meat curls up, away from shells. Serve hot
with lemon juice dribbled on top (or offer garlic butter for dipping, a
variation known as Paddler's Escargot).

**Note:** If limpets are so small they slip through grill, place them on a
bed of wet seaweed in a skillet and put the whole thing on the grill.

# Crab Omelet

**Serves:** 1
**Preparation time in camp:** 10 minutes

*This is an amiable answer to how to make the most of a little crab. To serve two people, make two separate omelets instead of doubling the recipe.*

2 eggs
¼ cup instant dry milk powder
1 tablespoon water
Dash cayenne pepper
Dash salt
Dash pepper
Pinch dill weed
Pinch tarragon
½ cup fresh crab
2 teaspoons oil
½ cup grated Cheddar cheese

**In camp:** Beat eggs with milk powder and water. Add seasonings (which can be premeasured and bagged with milk powder at home). Stir in crab meat.

Heat oil in skillet and cook egg mixture over low heat, tilting pan and lifting cooked edges to let liquid run underneath. Sprinkle cheese over surface, cover, and cook until bottom is golden brown and top is set, but still somewhat creamy. Fold in half to serve.

**Variation:** Omit dill and tarragon; use ¼ cup chopped Vienna sausage or diced salami in place of crab.

# Prawn and Brie Omelet

**Serves:** 2
**Preparation time in camp:** 15 minutes

*An elegant dinner omelet makes the most of a few prawns. Serve with steamed asparagus or glasswort and warm chunks of sourdough bread.*

1 clove garlic, minced
Oil
4 or more cleaned prawns or large shrimp
¼ teaspoon thyme
6 fresh eggs, beaten
2¼ ounces (½ can) Brie cheese, cubed

**In camp:** In nonstick-coated skillet, sauté garlic in oil until golden. Add prawns, stir to coat with oil, and sauté a few minutes (until meat is no longer translucent). Sprinkle with thyme and pour in beaten egg. Lift edges of egg as it cooks, tilting pan until egg is no longer liquid. Scatter Brie evenly over surface, lower heat, and cover skillet for about 2 minutes. Fold omelet in half, cover skillet, remove from heat, and let stand about 2 minutes more as cheese continues to melt.

## Fresh Artichokes

**Serves:** 4
**Preparation time in camp:** 45 minutes

*If roughing it elegantly is your style, imagine watching the sun set while sipping a nice white wine (the bottle chilled in the bottom of the boat, of course) and dipping artichoke petals in lemon butter. Artichokes, despite their elegance, are stout travelers.*

6 quarts salted water
2 cloves garlic, halved lengthwise
1 fresh lemon
4 fresh artichokes
¼ pound butter

**In camp:** Bring water to boil, adding garlic. Squeeze lemon, reserving juice and adding rind to water in pot. Rinse artichokes and cut stem flush with bottom. Place in water, cover pot, and return to full boil. Uncover, reduce heat and simmer about 35 minutes, until bottom can be pierced with a fork. Use fork to lift and drain each artichoke. Let cool enough to handle. Meanwhile, melt butter in lemon juice. Serve each artichoke in an individual bowl. Dip into lemon butter.

# Roast Corn on the Cob

**Serves:** 4
**Preparation time in camp:** 30 minutes

*Kayakers often roast their corn because doing so takes not a drop of fresh water. (Consider roasting potatoes and/or a whole fresh fish in foil to go with the corn.)*

8 ears fresh corn
Butter
Salt and pepper

**In camp:** Trim stems and soak corn, husks and all, 1 hour in sea water. Lay on grill over hot coals and roast, turning frequently, 10 to 20 minutes. Serve with butter, salt and pepper.

# Roasted Potatoes

**Serves:** Any number
**Preparation time in camp:** 60 minutes

1 baking potato per person
Oil
Seasonings: butter, salt, pepper, sour cream sauce, plain yogurt,
     chopped green onion

**In camp:** Scrub potatoes and pare eyes or prick skin. Rub skin with oil, then wrap each potato in aluminum foil. Place on grill over coals and bake, turning and rearranging occasionally. Test for doneness by squeezing or piercing with fork. When tender, unwrap, slash tops and serve with seasonings.

# Roasted Potatoes with Onions

**Serves:** 6
**Preparation time in camp:** 1 hour

12 baking potatoes
2 onions, thinly sliced
½ cup (¼ pound) butter, melted (or 1 packet Butter Buds mixed with ½
    cup hot water)
Oil
1 package dry onion or leek soup mix

**In camp:** Scrub potatoes and slice each crosswise into 4 pieces.
Reassemble each potato on greased foil, placing an onion slice between
each piece of potato. Sprinkle soup mix evenly over all potatoes; pour
melted butter or substitute over potatoes. Fold foil to enclose each
potato securely. Roast on grill over coals, turning and rearranging
once or twice.

# Eternal Vegetables

**Serves:** 2
**Preparation time in camp:** 15 minutes

*Long-lasting vegetables are steamed in a fragrant sauce, excellent
spooned over rice and served as a side dish with fish. (Add chunks of
fish—fresh or leftover—along with the vegetable florets to make a main
dish.)*

1 clove garlic, minced
¼-inch slice ginger root, minced
½ onion, coarsely chopped
1 to 2 tablespoons oil
1 cup halved broccoli or cauliflower florets
1 green pepper, cut in julienne strips
1 chicken or vegetable bouillon cube, crumbled
2 tablespoons instant dry milk powder
½ packet Butter Buds
½ cup water

**In camp:** Sauté garlic, ginger, and onion in oil until onion is golden.
Add florets and green pepper; stir-fry 2 minutes. Stir bouillon, milk
powder, and Butter Buds into water and beat to blend well. Pour into
pan, cover, and steam over low heat until florets are fork-tender.

# Enough
# to Feed a
# Crowd

# Judy's Creative Bouillabaisse

**Serves:** 6 to 8
**Preparation time at home:** A few minutes
**Preparation time in camp:** 30 minutes

*On the day when the people on a kayak trip are really getting into fishing and foraging, Judy Moyer of Pacific Water Sports, Seattle, volunteers to cook. Reaching for two zip locking bags of premeasured ingredients, she stirs up a pot of fragrant broth in which the combined catch simmers to create a memorable meal.*

4 dried tomatoes, chopped
12 ounces (2 cans) tomato paste, dried into leather (see Index)
½ teaspoon garlic powder
1 tablespoon fennel seed
½ teaspoon saffron ("expensive, but worth it," Judy says)
2 bay leaves, crumbled
1 teaspoon dried, grated orange rind
⅛ teaspoon celery seed
3 tablespoons dried parsley flakes
1 teaspoon pepper
2 tablespoons salt
1 tablespoon dried onion
4 cups hot water
½ cup oil
3 pounds (or more) fresh seafood, the fish cleaned and cut into bite-size pieces, shellfish scrubbed but still in shells

**At home:** Pack dried tomatoes and tomato paste leather in one plastic bag; pack the rest of the dry ingredients in another.

**In camp:** Soak dried tomatoes and paste in hot water to reconstitute.
   In oil, sauté contents of dry ingredients packet. Combine with tomato mixture in a very large pot (this mixture has been known to exceed Dutch-oven capacity, and end up in a dishpan).
   Bring to boil and add seafood—"clams, cod, snapper, sea cucumber, a few scallops, lots of mussels, limpets." Simmer 15 to 20 minutes until seafood is done. Serve with fresh-baked cornbread.

**Variation 1:** Chop 1 fresh zucchini and 2 fresh onions; sauté with seasonings. Along with tomato mixture, add ½ cup white wine.

**Variation 2:** On the last night of a trip, collect and add to the pot the best fresh foods that everyone has left. "Every time I make this, it turns out different," Judy says. "It really lends itself to improvising—that's the creative part."

# Cioppino

**Serves: 8**
**Preparation time in camp:** 1 hour

*This easy-to-make version of cioppino, the tomato-rich Italian version of bouillabaisse, is fun to make with the combined catch of a group's fishing and clamming. To feed eight people you will need the equivalent of four pounds of fish and at least sixteen steamer clams. Do not hesitate to add cooked Dungeness crab or shrimp, scrubbed limpets or cockles, chopped sea cucumber or squid. The more mixed the bag, the better! (Bring a couple of cans of tuna or shrimp to add only if needed.)*

2 to 4 cloves garlic, minced
1 large onion, chopped
2 green bell peppers, diced
2 tablespoons olive oil
4 ounces (1 can) button mushroom caps
46 ounces (1 can) tomato juice
32 ounces (2 cans) Italian-style tomatoes
30 ounces (2 cans) chicken broth
1 teaspoon dried fennel
¼ cup dried parsley
4 pounds fish fillets, cubed
16 to 32 steamer clams, scrubbed

**In camp:** Sauté garlic, onion, and peppers in oil in bottom of large pot. Drain mushrooms and add. Stir in all other ingredients except seafood and simmer 45 minutes. Bring to boil and add fish and clams. Cover and cook about 10 minutes, until clam shells pop open.

# Austrian Cream Cheese Soup

**Serves:** 10 to 12
**Preparation time in camp:** 30 minutes

*This soup, popular with kayakers on trips with the Northwest Outdoor Center, based in Seattle, is an excellent dish to take to a potluck picnic. For best results, cook over a campfire or on a camp stove with a burner that spreads the flame. This is too big a batch to work well over the pinpoint flame of a backpacker's stove.*

6 tablespoons butter
6 green onions including greens, chopped
4 stalks celery, chopped
6 tablespoons flour
5 chicken bouillon cubes, crushed
7 cups water
1 pound cream cheese
2 cups plain yogurt
4 egg yolks, beaten
Freshly ground pepper to taste

**In camp:** Melt butter in large pot over medium heat. Add white part of onions (reserving chopped greens for garnish) and celery; sauté until they are transparent. Stir in flour and let it bubble together with butter 2 minutes, stirring occasionally; do not brown. Add crushed bouillon cubes and water. Bring to boil, stirring occasionally. Lower heat and simmer partially covered for 15 minutes.

In small pot, slightly warm cream cheese and yogurt. Add egg yolks and beat all together until smooth. (A whisk is handy for that.) Gradually add 2 cups bouillon mixture, blending well. Add to remainder of bouillon mixture in large pot and stir over low heat until soup is heated through; do not boil. Sprinkle chopped onion greens on top.

# Orcas Island Pasta Salad

**Serves:** 8
**Preparation time in camp:** 30 minutes

*This hearty, main-dish salad was invented by Frieda Cron when she
and her husband Kevin lived on Orcas Island in the San Juan Islands
of Washington State. Start with fresh, frozen, or canned vegetables, or
some of each. Serve with jug wine, crusty French bread and butter, and
pass the cracked black pepper.*

12 ounces rotini (corkscrew macaroni)
Water
3 cups vegetables (choose combination of peas, sliced green beans,
    broccoli or cauliflower florets)
2 handfuls fresh mushrooms, sliced
1 small can black olives, sliced in half and drained
1 teaspoon basil
1 teaspoon oregano
8 ounces (1 bottle) Parmesan salad dressing
12 ounces ham, cut in bite-size pieces
½ cup grated sharp Cheddar cheese
Salt and pepper to taste

**In camp:** Cook rotini in boiling salted water about 10 minutes (until
tender). Drain. Rinse to chill, if desired. Meanwhile, prepare
vegetables, cooking them together with sliced mushrooms in small
amount of salted water until tender-crisp. Drain. Stir over cold water
to chill, if desired. Combine all ingredients in large bowl or pot. Serve
either warm or chilled.

# Corn and Tomato Salad

**Serves:** 8
**Preparation time in camp:** 15 minutes

*Here is a salad with which to surprise kayaking companions who thought all of the fresh food was gone. You can carry all ingredients for several days and put them together in minutes. (For extra convenience, carry premeasured dressing ingredients in a plastic bottle from home.)*

24 ounces (1 can) whole-kernel corn, drained
½ bunch (about 4) green onions including greens, chopped
½ basket cherry tomatoes, halved
⅓ cup oil
3 tablespoons vinegar
1 tablespoon Dijon or similar mustard
1 teaspoon basil
Salt and pepper to taste

**In camp:** Combine corn, onions, and tomatoes. In bottle or jar, shake together remaining ingredients and pour over vegetables. Toss gently and serve.

# Five Bean Salad

**Serves:** 8
**Preparation time in camp:** 15 minutes plus standing time

*Here is a popular salad to make in the morning, marinate while paddling, and serve at night. (Or make it at home, chill overnight, insulate and carry to serve in the evening.)*

16 ounces (1 can) green beans
16 ounces (1 can) yellow wax beans
16 ounces (1 can) kidney beans
16 ounces (1 can) lima beans
16 ounces (1 can) garbanzos
1 medium onion, chopped
1 green pepper, diced
½ cup oil
⅔ cup cider vinegar
½ cup sugar
1 teaspoon salt

**In camp:** Rinse and drain all beans. Combine with onion and green pepper. In bottle or jar, combine oil, vinegar, sugar, and salt; shake until sugar is dissolved. Pour over beans. Chill 8 hours or overnight, stirring once to marinate evenly.

## Trudi's Tortillas

**Yield:** About 30 tortillas
**Preparation time in camp:** 45 minutes to prepare, 1 hour to cook

*Trudi Angell of Paddling South, leader of kayak trips in the Sea of Cortez, makes her own tortillas from scratch (which never fails to amaze gringo paddlers).*

3 cups white flour
3 cups whole wheat flour
¾ cup vegetable shortening
2½ cups hot water
1 teaspoon salt

**In camp:** Set aside "a handful or two" of the flours, and mix the rest with shortening. Add water "not so hot that you cannot touch it" and salt. Mix and knead until dough forms a ball, adding the reserved flour as needed.

Knead about 10 minutes more, until dough is smooth. Tear off and roll pieces of dough about the size of golf balls. Let dough rest 15 to 20 minutes.

Then "roll it out and start flapping," says Trudi, describing the traditional Mexican method of flattening the balls of dough into circles.

Heat a lightly greased skillet. Fry each tortilla 30 seconds, then flip and cook 45 seconds to 1 minute. Flip a second time and cook 30 seconds more. The finished tortilla should be flour colored with little brown dots speckled over both sides; that takes a hot skillet and very little grease.

# Dinners
# That
# Travel
# up to
# a Week

# Stir-fry Supper

**Serves:** 6 to 8
**Preparation time in camp:** 30 minutes to prepare vegetables, 10 minutes to cook

*The flavor of the toasted sesame oil makes a memorable difference. (Carry it in a 35-millimeter film canister along with ginger grated at home.)*

2 tablespoons salad oil
2 tablespoons toasted sesame oil
1-inch piece fresh ginger, peeled and grated
2 cloves garlic, minced
1 onion, coarsely chopped
1 cup whole raw cashews or slivered almonds
2 carrots, cut diagonally into ¼-inch slices
2 ribs celery, sliced diagonally into ½-inch pieces
1 green pepper, cut into strips
½ pound fresh mushrooms, sliced
1 small zucchini, sliced diagonally
½ pound snow peas (or 1 package frozen)
1 small bunch bok choy, cut crosswise at 1-inch intervals
8 to 10 ounces firm tofu, cubed
Juice of ½ lemon (1 tablespoon or more)
Cooked rice
Soy sauce

**In camp:** Heat oils, ginger, and garlic in wok or large skillet. Add onion, cashews, carrots, and celery; stir-fry about 4 minutes. Add green pepper, mushrooms, zucchini, and snow peas; stir-fry about 2 minutes more. Stir in bok choy and tofu. Steam until hot and tender, about 5 minutes more. Drizzle with lemon juice and toss. Serve with hot rice and soy sauce.

# Shiitake Stir-Fry

**Serves:** 2
**Preparation time in camp:** 30 minutes to prepare vegetables, 10 minutes to cook

*The distinctive, delicious flavor of dried shiitake mushrooms makes this a special dish. All ingredients are durable travelers, so you can enjoy this many days after leaving port.*

6 dried shiitake mushrooms, presoaked 30 minutes
1 clove garlic, minced
1 onion, chopped
1 tablespoon oil
1 tablespoon toasted sesame oil
1 carrot, sliced diagonally into ¼-inch pieces
1 tablespoon dried parsley flakes
10½ ounces fresh tofu, cubed, or 1 package freeze-dried chicken
    chunks, reconstituted
½ head green cabbage, coarsely chopped
1 tablespoon cornstarch (optional)
Cooked rice
Soy sauce to taste

**In camp:** Squeeze moisture from mushrooms, reserving liquid. Cut away and discard hard stem. Slice mushroom caps into bite-size pieces.

In wok or large skillet, sauté garlic and onion in oils. Add carrot pieces and stir-fry about 2 minutes. Add mushrooms, parsley, and tofu and gently stir-fry about 2 minutes longer. Fold in cabbage. Add about 2 tablespoons mushroom soaking water, cover, and steam about 5 minutes—just until cabbage is tender-crisp.

Add cornstarch to about ½ cup remaining mushroom soaking water and shake or beat to blend. Pour into wok and stir to thicken sauce. Serve immediately with rice and soy sauce.

# Chile Rellenos Casserole

**Serves:** 4
**Preparation time in camp:** 60 minutes

*This one is a slow cooker, ideal for a Dutch oven, reflector oven, or improvisation with coals to help a covered pot cook evenly from all sides. Munch on tortilla chips (perhaps with salsa or guacamole dip) while you are waiting; serve with Spanish Rice.*

4 ounces (1 can) whole green chilies
¾ pound jack cheese
2 eggs
½ cup milk
¼ cup flour
½ teaspoon salt

**In camp:** Rinse chilies, tearing to flatten and removing seeds. Cut cheese into slices about ¼ inch thick. Grease Dutch oven or line pot with foil and grease. Place half of cheese in bottom. Cover with layer of chilies, then top with remaining cheese. Beat eggs, blending in milk, flour, and salt. Pour over cheese and chilies. Cover and bake over medium heat about 45 minutes, or until edges are browned and center is custardlike.

# Spanish Rice

**Serves: 4**
**Preparation time in camp:** 30 to 50 minutes (varies with white or
    brown rice)

2 tablespoons oil
2 cloves garlic, minced
1 medium onion, chopped
1 green bell pepper, diced
1 cup uncooked rice
16 ounces (1 can) tomatoes with basil
1¾ cups water (estimated)
1 teaspoon chili powder
½ teaspoon cumin
½ cup beef-flavored TVP (textured vegetable protein), optional
Salt and pepper

**In camp:** In large skillet, wok, or pot, heat oil and sauté garlic, onion, and pepper. Stir in rice.
    Drain tomatoes, saving liquid. Add tomatoes to mixture in pan, chopping coarsely with spoon.
    Add water to liquid drained from tomatoes to total 2 cups. Add chili powder and cumin. Bring to boil and simmer, covered, until liquid is absorbed and rice is done. Stir in TVP (if desired), salt and pepper to taste. Heat 5 minutes more.

# Tamale Pie

**Serves:** 6
**Preparation time in camp:** 20 minutes with cornmeal, 10 minutes with masa

*For easy cleanup, use foil to line a Dutch oven, wok, or large pot. If you choose the latter, use a skillet for browning the onions and meat, then combine with other ingredients in the foil-lined pot. Serve with green salad.*

1 onion, chopped
1 pound lean ground beef
2 tablespoons oil
16 ounces (1 can) stewed tomatoes
17 ounces (1 can) whole kernel corn, undrained
1 cup sour cream
1 cup cornmeal or masa
14 ounces pitted ripe olives
2 teaspoons salt
1 tablespoon chili powder
½ teaspoon cumin
2 cups jack cheese, shredded

**In camp:** Lightly brown chopped onion and ground beef in oil. Add all other ingredients except cheese. Stir until thoroughly mixed. Sprinkle with cheese, cover and simmer until done.

**Note:** For a longer-lasting meal package, substitute TVP (textured vegetable protein) for the ground beef.

# Lazy Enchiladas

**Serves:** 2 generously
**Preparation time in camp:** 1 hour

*These enchiladas are "lazy" because ingredients are layered in the pot instead of rolled in tortillas. For best results, cook over a campfire for slow, even heating. Bake in a greased Dutch oven, foil-lined cooking pot, or flat-bottomed wok.*

2 tablespoons instant dry milk powder
¼ cup dried onion flakes
½ cup grated Cheddar cheese
10 ounces (1 can) mild enchilada sauce
1 packet sour cream sauce mix
½ pound jack cheese
5 ounces (1 can) chicken (or 1 package freeze-dried chicken)
3½ ounces (1 can) pitted black olives
6 corn tortillas
2 green onions, chopped (optional)

**At home:** Bag together milk powder and onion flakes. Bag grated Cheddar cheese. For long trips, dry enchilada sauce (following directions for Tomato Sauce Leather), olives, and grated cheeses.

**In camp:** In small pot, combine sour cream sauce mix, milk powder, and onion flakes, adding water as specified on sauce mix packet. Set aside to rehydrate and blend, about 10 minutes. Meanwhile, heat enchilada sauce with water in lid of large pot and slice jack cheese as thinly as possible.

To sour cream sauce, add chicken and olives. Tear tortillas in half.

Spread about ½ cup enchilada sauce in bottom of large cooking pot. Place 4 tortilla halves overlapping on top of that, and spread half of sour cream mixture over them. Top with ½ of the jack cheese. Repeat layers, ending with last 4 tortilla halves. Pour remaining enchilada sauce over all. Sprinkle Cheddar cheese on top, cover and simmer 30 to 45 minutes.

To serve, spoon through all layers. Sprinkle each serving with chopped green onion, if desired.

# Beachiladas

**Serves:** 6
**Preparation time in camp:** 30 minutes to prepare for buffet-style
  serving, 30 more minutes to heat and serve tortillas

*A specialty of David Arcese, Beachiladas are popular with kayakers on
guided trips with Northern Lights Expeditions.*

2 pounds (2 cans) refried beans
1 pound (1 can) red kidney beans or pinto beans
24 ounces (2 or 3 jars) salsa (divided)
1 head iceberg lettuce, chopped
3 fresh tomatoes, chopped
1 onion, chopped
½ pound Cheddar cheese, shredded
16 ounces (1 can) pitted black olives, whole or sliced
1 cup sour cream, fresh or made from sour cream sauce mix (optional)
12 large tortillas made of white or whole wheat (not corn)

**In camp:** Heat together refried beans, kidney beans, and 8 ounces
(1 cup) of the salsa.
  Spread out for self-service the remaining salsa, lettuce, tomatoes,
onion, cheese, olives, sour cream (if desired), and heated bean mixture.
  Heat tortillas one at a time in hot, dry skillet. Each takes about 1
minute, 30 seconds on each side. Serve straight from the skillet for
people to fill with bean mixture and choice of toppings; roll up burrito-
style to eat.

# Bill's Burritos

**Yield:** 4 big burritos
**Preparation time in camp:** 15 minutes

*These big, warm burritos are easy to make with refried beans straight
from the can. On longer trips where bulk is a consideration, dry the
canned beans at home and reconstitute in the skillet as they heat (or
buy a dried frijoles mix).*

15 ounces (1 can) refried beans with green chilies
Water
4 flour tortillas
6 ounces jack or Gouda cheese, slivered
½ cup fresh onion, chopped
Salsa or chopped tomato (optional)

**In camp:** Heat beans in pot, thinning with a little water if needed to prevent sticking. Place one tortilla at a time over top of the same pot with edges of tortilla hanging down over sides. Cover with lid and steam over beans a minute or two to warm. Fill first tortilla as second one heats, then fill second and eat while warm. Repeat with third and fourth tortillas.

To fill, spread ¼ of beans in strip down center of tortilla. Top beans with ¼ of cheese, onion, and salsa (if desired). Roll up tortilla to enclose filling.

## Spicy Sausage Supper

**Serves:** 2 to 4
**Preparation time in camp:** 90 minutes

1 cup lentils, washed
3 cups water
2 onions, chopped
½ pound fresh mushrooms, halved
1 pound cooked Kielbasa sausages, cut in 1-inch pieces
3 tablespoons oil
1 to 2 teaspoons curry powder
½ teaspoon pepper
1 tablespoon dried parsley flakes
1 cup sour cream (or sour cream sauce)
4 green onions, chopped

**In camp:** Bring lentils and water to boil, reduce heat, cover and simmer 40 minutes. Meanwhile, sauté onion, mushrooms, and sausage pieces in oil until vegetables are golden. Drain off any excess oil. Combine with lentils, stirring in curry powder, pepper, and parsley flakes. Cover and simmer (or simply hold over low heat) 30 minutes. Serve topped with sour cream and green onion.

## Skillet Frank Supper

**Serves:** 4
**Preparation time in camp:** 25 minutes

1 cup uncooked white rice
8 ounces (1 can) sauerkraut
¼ cup ketchup
2 cups water
8 frankfurters

**In camp:** Stir together in large skillet (or cooking pot) rice, sauerkraut, ketchup, and water. Bring to boil. Reduce heat, cover, and simmer 10 minutes. Add franks (whole or cut in chunks). Continue to simmer about 10 minutes longer, until rice is done and franks are hot.

## Cheese Fondue

**Serves:** 6
**Preparation time in camp:** 30 minutes

*This fondue is the "Saturday dinner special" of Rana Fitzsimmons-Wilcox who has been leading kayak trips for Spirit Tours.*

28 ounces (2 foil packets) fondue mix (including cheese and seasonings)
1 pound Swiss cheese, diced
32 ounces (2 cans) baby potatoes
2 large bunches fresh broccoli
2 loaves French bread, sliced

**In camp:** Place unopened packets of fondue mix in hot water and simmer to heat.

Cut potatoes and broccoli into bite-size pieces.

Pour heated fondue mix into skillet with nonstick coating. Add Swiss cheese; heat and stir until melted and blended with mix.

To eat, use forks or bamboo skewers to dip pieces of potato, broccoli, and French bread into hot fondue.

# Eggs Internationale

**Serves:** 2
**Preparation time in camp:** 15 minutes

*This unusual combination of ingredients is the stuff of which gourmet reputations are made. Serve with long grain and wild rice with herbs and seasonings.*

6 ounces (1 can) chicken
4 ounces (1 can) artichoke hearts, drained
2 to 3 ounces feta cheese, crumbled
¼ teaspoon thyme
6 fresh eggs, beaten
Salt and cracked black pepper

**In camp:** Drain chicken, reserving oil. Heat about 1 tablespoon of the oil in skillet and sauté chicken until heated. Stir in artichoke hearts and sauté about 2 minutes. Sprinkle feta cheese and thyme over chicken and artichoke hearts; fold together. Pour in beaten eggs. Lift edges of egg and tilt pan until egg is no longer liquid. Cover skillet and cook over low, even heat about 2 minutes. Uncover, fold omelet in half, cover and set aside about 2 minutes more. Season with salt and pepper to taste.

# Hearty Potato Chowder

**Serves:** 4
**Preparation time in camp:** 20 to 30 minutes

1 onion, chopped
1 bell pepper (green or red), diced
2 tablespoons oil
12 ounces (1 can) whole kernel corn
1 package dry potato soup mix
Water and/or milk as specified on soup mix packet
4 ounces (1 deli package) smoked, cooked ham, cubed

**In camp:** In pot, sauté onion and pepper in oil. Drain the corn, reserving liquid, and add to onion and pepper. Stir in dry soup mix and gradually add water and/or milk as specified on soup mix packet; use liquid from corn as part of the total amount. Cook 20 minutes, stirring occasionally. Add ham and cook 10 minutes longer.

# Tabbouli Salad

**Serves:** 2 to 4 as main dish, 4 to 6 as side dish
**Preparation time in camp:** 20 minutes (plus standing time)

*A salad you can prepare after most of the fresh food is gone, this*
*traditional Middle Eastern dish tastes best when the lemon and mint*
*have had a chance to permeate the wheat. Mix it in the morning and let*
*it ride and chill all day against the bottom of the boat. Serve with split*
*pea soup (made from a dry mix), and dinner is ready with a minimum*
*of fixing. (As an alternative, mix Tabbouli Salad at home, chill*
*overnight, insulate and carry to serve with dinner that night. Double or*
*triple the recipe to serve a crowd.)*

2 cups boiling water
1 cup bulgur cracked wheat
½ cup lemon juice
½ cup oil
1 teaspoon salt
1 teaspoon pepper
2 tablespoons dried parsley flakes
2 teaspoons dried mint, crumbled
1 bunch green onions, chopped
2 tomatoes, diced

**In camp:** Pour boiling water over bulgur and let stand 1 hour; drain.
Add all other ingredients and stir together, blending well. Chill several
hours, stirring once or twice to marinate evenly throughout.

# Thanksgiving Dinner

**Serves:** 4
**Preparation time at home:** 10 minutes
**Preparation time in camp:** 90 minutes

*Taking the Thanksgiving turkey on a camping trip is a tradition*
*dating back more than twenty years in my family. In mild-winter*
*regions such as Puget Sound and the San Juan Islands, the four-day*
*Thanksgiving holiday offers the prospect of pleasant off-season kayaking*
*and camping in state parks that you are likely to have to yourself.*

½ split turkey (about 6 pounds)
Oil or shortening
Salt and pepper
1 package top-of-stove stuffing mix
1 package freeze-dried peas
1 package turkey gravy mix
1 can cranberry sauce

**At home:** Order a fresh hen turkey split in half lengthwise (like a chicken split for the barbecue grill) and frozen. Discuss this with butcher well in advance, as it usually takes at least a week's lead time. (Cutting a frozen turkey with a band saw is possible, but mentioned only as a last-ditch option. You have to keep stopping the saw and brushing frozen turkey "sawdust" from the teeth of the blade, and the turkey will make a break for freedom each time you restart the cut. Far better to have the butcher special-order and cut a fresh turkey, then freeze and wrap it for you to carry.)

**In camp:** Secure skin along cut edge of breast with small skewers (sold in package for use with turkey). Rub thawed (or almost-thawed) turkey with oil or shortening and season with salt and pepper. Grill on rack over coals, covering loosely with a tent of foil to help hold in heat, and turning several times. (Do not pierce bird with fork, which lets juices escape.) Remove foil and baste with additional oil or shortening to finish browning. Total cooking time is usually 60 to 90 minutes.

　　Ideally, use a second fire as a continuing source of coals to maintain even heat for bird and over which to cook stuffing, peas, and gravy during the final 20 minutes of turkey-grilling time. Charcoal briquets for both fires make it easy to succeed with this "production number."

**Variation:** Order a precooked, smoked turkey or portion thereof, (usually) vacuum-packed. Unwrap and grill as described until heated through, which usually takes about 45 minutes.

**Caution:** Never carry a half-cooked turkey or one already prepared with stuffing. To do so is an open invitation to food poisoning.

# Dinners to Eat after a Week

## Sea Kayakers' Spaghetti

**Serves:** 3
**Preparation time in camp:** 20 minutes

*This is the recipe that prompted Randy Washburne to mutter happily through a mouthful, "I would even eat this stuff at home." (That particular batch was made with Lawry's Spaghetti Sauce Mix.)*

6 ounces rotini (spiral-shaped pasta)
1½ ounces (1 packet) spaghetti sauce mix
1 ounce Parmesan cheese, grated
8 ounces (1 can) tomato sauce
3 to 5 ounces (1 can) pitted black olives
3 cups water

**At home:** Measure rotini into plastic bag along with spaghetti sauce packet. Measure cheese into a sandwich bag and close with twist-tie;

enclose in larger plastic bag. Pack with cans of tomato sauce and olives.

**In camp:** In small pot, stir together tomato sauce and contents of spaghetti sauce packet. Gradually add water, stirring to blend. Bring to boil, then reduce heat and simmer (or simply keep warm) 30 minutes. During that time, drain olives, discarding liquid. Add olives (whole or cut in halves) to spaghetti sauce.

Meanwhile, in large pot, bring salted water to boil and cook rotini until done (about 10 minutes). Drain.

Serve rotini topped with spaghetti sauce and pass Parmesan cheese to sprinkle on top. Garlic Toast goes very well with it, too.

**Variations:** Add ¼ cup TVP (textured vegetable protein) and/or dried vegetables (such as home-dried zucchini or store-bought green bell pepper flakes) to the simmering sauce.

**Note:** A much more compact and lightweight package suitable for taking on extended trips can be made by home-drying the tomato sauce and olives.

# Garlic Toast

**Serves:** 2
**Preparation time in camp:** 5 minutes per muffin

*Indestructible English muffins make Garlic Toast possible a week or more after the French bread has disappeared.*

2 English muffins
2 tablespoons butter or margarine
¼ teaspoon garlic powder

**In camp:** Split muffins into halves. Spread with butter or margarine and sprinkle with garlic powder.

Heat muffin halves in skillet, first warming the muffin bottoms and then turning to fry the buttered tops until golden brown.

# Mac and Cheese

**Serves:** 2
**Preparation time in camp:** 20 minutes

*Nice and sloppy and full of flavor, this beats any of the prepackaged mixes you can buy.*

6 ounces elbow macaroni
1 packet cheese sauce mix
1 packet sour cream sauce mix
½ cup dry milk powder
1 tablespoon dried onion flakes
1 tablespoon dried parsley flakes
Water
Salt to taste

**At home:** Measure macaroni and place in plastic bag along with the two unopened sauce mix packets. Measure milk powder into sandwich bag, twist and close with twist-tie. Measure onion and parsley into same sandwich bag above the tie. Close top with a second twist-tie. Put sandwich bag into larger plastic bag with the rest.

**In camp:** In large pot, bring salted water to boil. Stir in macaroni and cook until tender (about 5 minutes), stirring occasionally.

Meanwhile, put onion and parsley flakes into small pot with contents of cheese sauce packet. Add the 1½ cups water a little at a time, stirring to blend. Heat, stirring, until sauce is smooth and hot. Add the sour cream sauce mix and dry milk. Mix well and heat just to boiling. Cover and set aside.

Drain water from macaroni. Combine macaroni with sauce.

# Mac and Cheese Deluxe

**Serves:** 2
**Preparation time in camp:** 45 minutes

*To make this deluxe version, you will need the basic ingredients for Mac and Cheese (preceding) plus:*

14 ounces (1 can) whole tomatoes, drained and cut in halves
¼ cup (about half of a 3-ounce can) HyGrade's West Virginia Brand
    real crumbled bacon
4 ounces cheese (any kind), grated or sliced thin

**In camp:** When macaroni is done, stir it into the sauce in small pot.
Rinse large pot and line with foil. Pour in ⅓ of macaroni mixture and
spread over it ½ of the tomatoes and bacon bits; repeat. Cover with
remaining macaroni mixture and top with sliced cheese. Cover and
keep over low heat 20 to 30 minutes.
    When serving, scoop through all layers.

**Note:** For a more compact, lighter weight package, substitute dried
whole tomatoes or tomato slices for the canned tomatoes.

# Coleslaw

**Serves:** 4
**Preparation time in camp:** 40 minutes

*Fresh green vegetables are the stuff of which fantasies are made when
the last provisioning point lies a week or more astern. Home-dried
cabbage springs to life to satisfy that craving in this crispy dish.*

1 small head cabbage (green, red, or half-and-half), shredded and dried
    (see Index)
1 tablespoon cider vinegar
1 tablespoon oil
½ teaspoon salt
1 tablespoon cold water
1 tablespoon dried parsley flakes
1 tablespoon dried onion flakes

**At home:** Pack the dried cabbage, parsley, and onion flakes in a
plastic bag; enclose film canister containing vinegar, oil, salt, and
water.

**In camp:** Soak cabbage in cold water about 30 minutes to
reconstitute. Drain off water; squeeze excess from cabbage. Shake
film canister and pour dressing over cabbage. Toss and serve.

## Uncle Ben's Almond Chicken

**Serves:** 2 to 4
**Preparation time in camp:** 50 minutes

*To serve two, make this recipe with one can of chicken. To serve four, add the second can of chicken and a side dish. Freeze-dried peas go very well with it, as does Swedish Fruit Soup for dessert.*

6 ounces (1 package) long grain and wild rice with herbs and
    seasonings
¼ cup dried onion flakes
¼ cup dried parsley flakes
¼ cup dried green bell pepper flakes (optional)
½ cup blanched, slivered almonds
6 or 12 ounces (1 or 2 cans) chicken
8 ounces (1 can) sliced, peeled water chestnuts

**At home:** Place rice and its packet of seasonings in a large plastic bag along with instructions from back of box. Measure dried vegetable flakes into small plastic bag and close with twist-tie. Put almonds, if not sealed in packet, into small plastic bag. Add almonds and vegetable flakes to large plastic bag, and seal. Pack with cans of chicken and water chestnuts.

**In camp:** In large pot, prepare rice according to package directions, adding dried vegetables along with rice seasonings.

Open cans, draining water chestnuts (but not chicken). Five minutes before end of cooking time, add water chestnuts and chicken to rice mixture, breaking chicken into chunks. Return pot to heat. When heated through, serve topped with almonds.

**Variation:** Substitute 6 ounces (1 can) tuna, drained, for chicken.

**Note:** To make a more compact, lighter weight package, carry freeze-dried chicken chunks to use in place of canned chicken. Sliced water chestnuts can be dehydrated at home (or omitted).

# Sherried Chicken Stew

**Serves:** 2
**Preparation time in camp:** 45 minutes

1 package dry mushroom soup mix
1 package freeze-dried diced chicken
1 package freeze-dried peas
¼ cup dried onion flakes
¼ cup dried parsley flakes
3 cups water (more as needed)
Sherry

**At home:** Remove packet of soup mix from carton and place in plastic bag with chicken, peas, onion flakes, and parsley flakes.

**In camp:** Bring to boil 3 cups water. Stir in all ingredients but soup mix, cover, and let stand about 20 minutes. Stir in soup mix. Return to heat and simmer, stirring occasionally, for about 10 minutes. Add water as needed to give mixture the consistency of stew. The crowning touch of flavor and fragrance is a splash of sherry stirred into each serving.

# Split Pea Souper

**Yield:** 4 1-cup servings
**Preparation time in camp:** 1 hour if peas presoaked

*Split peas come in several colors, including yellow and red in addition to the usual green. Use all of one color or mix them as you please for subtle differences in flavor and shade.*

1 cup split peas
1 chicken bouillon cube
¼ cup dry vegetable soup mix (sold in bulk, it usually runs heavily to
    carrots and celery)
1 tablespoon dried onion flakes
1 teaspoon dried parsley flakes
1 teaspoon rosemary, crushed
½ teaspoon thyme
¼ teaspoon garlic powder
1 bay leaf
½ cup salami, cut into bite-size pieces
5 cups hot water (divided)
Salt and cracked black pepper to taste
Bacon bits (fresh or canned) to sprinkle on top

**At home:** Measure peas into plastic bag. Enclose packet containing all other dry ingredients. Do not preslice salami. Separately wrap it (if it is not sealed in store packaging) and enclose.

**In camp:** Right after breakfast, pour peas into wide-mouth poly bottle and add 2 cups hot water. Cap tightly and let soak all day to shorten cooking time by 20 minutes or more.

    To cook, pour contents of bottle into large pot. Add 3 more cups water and bring to boil, stirring in dry ingredients and salami. Simmer about 45 minutes, until peas are soft. (This will take more than an hour if the peas have not been presoaked for at least 3 hours.) Season with salt and pepper and serve garnished with bacon bits.

# Peppi Potatoes

**Serves:** 2
**Preparation time in camp:** 1 hour

*Simple and satisfying, this dinner goes well with a salad or side dish of beach greens gathered while the pot is simmering.*

5 ounces (1 package) dry scalloped potato mix
Instant dry milk powder, if needed
3 ounces pepperoni
Boiling water

**At home:** Repackage dry potatoes and their packet of seasonings in plastic bag along with instructions from cardboard box. If those instructions call for milk, measure milk powder into small plastic bag (4 tablespoons milk powder for each cup of milk), and enclose.

**In camp:** Slice pepperoni into bite-size pieces and put into large, foil-lined pot with dry potatoes and seasonings. Add boiling water (and/or milk in amount specified) and simmer over coals or low heat 45 minutes or until done.

**Variations:** Serve topped with 2 fresh green onions, chopped tops and all, when available. Substitute 6 ounces deviled ham for pepperoni, or, substitute dry potatoes au gratin mix for scalloped potato mix.

# Lentil Chili

**Serves: 2**
**Preparation time in camp: 45 minutes**

*Warm, buttered cornbread is especially good with chili. This combination also gives you grain and legumes in the same meal, boosting the nutritional value as explained in the chapter, "Food to Paddle On."*

⅔ cup lentils
1 tablespoon dried onion flakes
1 tablespoon dried parsley flakes
2 teaspoons chili powder
¼ teaspoon cumin
¾ teaspoon oregano
¼ teaspoon garlic powder
½ teaspoon salt
½ cup whole dried tomatoes
3 cups water

**At home:** Wash lentils and dry thoroughly. Combine in plastic bag with all ingredients except tomatoes (enclose them in a sandwich bag) and water.

**In camp:** Stir lentil mixture into 3 cups water. Bring to boil, reduce heat, and simmer 15 minutes, stirring occasionally. Add tomatoes and simmer 15 minutes more.

# Chili con Corny

**Serves: 2**
**Preparation time in camp: 20 minutes**

*Jiffy Cornbread Cakes go well with a pot of chili. Consider frying a batch while the chili heats.*

15 ounces (1 can) chili with beans
7 to 8 ounces (1 can) corn, either whole kernel or cream style
3 tablespoons dried onion flakes or ½ medium onion
4 ounces (1 deli packet) grated Cheddar cheese

**In camp:** In large pot, combine chili and corn. If using dried onion flakes, stir them in. Heat thoroughly.

Sprinkle grated cheese on top, cover, and set aside to let cheese melt.

Meanwhile, if using fresh onion, chop to sprinkle on top of individual servings.

**Note:** For a more compact package to carry, combine beans and corn at home, then dehydrate and crumble into plastic bag. In camp, add dried onion and water. Heat, stirring occasionally, to reconstitute. Top with slivers of cheese from lunch sack.

## Camping Curry

**Serves:** 2
**Preparation time in camp:** 20 minutes

1½ cups TVP (textured vegetable protein)
2 teaspoons chicken bouillon granules
¼ cup dried onion flakes
1 package freeze-dried peas
1½ cups instant rice
1 packet Butter Buds
1 package S & B curry sauce mix (medium hot)
5½ cups water (divided)

**At home:** Measure and package together TVP, bouillon granules, onion flakes, and peas. Measure and package together rice and Butter Buds. Enclose both packets in bag with curry sauce mix (removed from box but left in airtight liner package).

**In camp:** Crumble curry mix into 2 cups hot water; stir to blend. Add contents of TVP packet and enough water (1 to 2 cups) to rehydrate without making sauce thin and runny. Heat, stirring occasionally. Set aside.

Stir rice mixture into 1½ cups boiling water. Cover and set aside 5 minutes. Fluff with fork. Serve topped with curry.

# Rice Curry

**Serves:** 2
**Preparation time in camp:** 30 minutes

*This wonderful sticky-rice version of curry can be eaten with chopsticks.*

1 cup short-grain or pearl rice
2 tablespoons dried onion flakes
2½ teaspoons curry powder
½ teaspoon celery salt
2 tablespoons slivered almonds
2 tablespoons raw cashews
¼ cup raisins
6 dried apricot halves, snipped into bits
6 dried apple rings, snipped into bits
¼ cup shredded unsweetened coconut
3 cups water
Chutney (optional)

**At home:** Measure rice into plastic bag. Enclose three separate packets: one containing onion flakes, curry powder, and celery salt; one containing nuts and fruits; one holding coconut.

**In camp:** Bring 3 cups water to boil. Stir in rice and contents of seasonings packet. Cover and simmer 15 minutes. Stir in nuts and fruits, cover, and simmer 5 minutes more. Serve with coconut sprinkled on top and chutney, if desired.

# "Mindless Meals," Extra Easy to Fix

# Royal Ramen

**Serves:** 1
**Preparation time in camp:** 10 minutes

*Simple to fix and satisfying, this is the supper to fix the night you stagger out on the beach, dog-tired from traveling, and wanting nothing more than to have a bite to eat and crash in your sleeping bag. I like to buy different flavors of ramen-type noodle dinners and prepackage the extra ingredients to have on hand.*

1 tablespoon dried onion flakes
1 tablespoon dried parsley flakes
¼ package freeze-dried green peas
4 tablespoons dried egg powder
1 package ramen-type noodle dinner
Water

**At home:** Measure onion flakes, parsley flakes, and peas into a plastic-wrapped packet. Measure egg powder into another one. Bag together with ramen-type noodle dinner.

**In camp:** Bring to boil the amount of water specified on noodle package. Add noodles and packet of dried vegetables. Simmer 4 minutes, until noodles are tender. Stir in seasonings from noodle dinner.

In bowl, beat together egg powder and an equal amount of water. Pour egg mixture into simmering pot of noodles. As egg starts to solidify, give it a stir or two to string it through the mixture.

**Variation:** Instead of egg powder, enclose 3 rectangles of dried tofu. Break tofu into bite-size pieces and add along with the noodles.

# Tortellini Supper

**Serves:** 2
**Preparation time in camp:** 20 minutes

*Running a close second to Royal Ramen in the simple-minded-supper department is this dinner for two. Of the several kinds of tortellini, we prefer the spinach pasta stuffed with cheese.*

1 tablespoon grated Parmesan cheese
1 tablespoon dried onion flakes
½ teaspoon fines herbes
1 cube chicken bouillon, crumbled
1 packet dry sour cream sauce mix
7 ounces (1 package) dry tortellini
Water

**At home:** Package Parmesan cheese in its own plastic packet. Combine onion flakes, fines herbes, and bouillon in another. Enclose both in zip locking bag with sour cream sauce packet and tortellini.

**In camp:** Bring to boil amount of water specified on tortellini package. Add seasonings and tortellini; simmer until pasta is tender. Meanwhile, add water to sour cream sauce mix and stir until blended. Let stand 10 minutes.

Serve tortellini with cooking broth. Top each serving with sour cream sauce and a sprinkling of Parmesan cheese.

## Stupid Pigeon Dinner

**Serves:** 4 (2 2-serving prepackaged dinners)
**Preparation time in camp:** 20 minutes

*This tasty, one-pot combination of chicken and rice originally was called the "Shearwater Dinner"—for diving birds of the North Pacific coast and the kayak design that bears their name. Then a kayaker who works with Russian fishermen in the Bering Sea reported that the Russian word for "shearwater" literally translates into English as "stupid pigeon." Instantly and irrevocably, the name of this "mindless meal" changed.*

6¼ ounces (2 packages) quick-cooking long grain and wild rice with
    herbs and seasoning
1 package freeze-dried diced chicken
1 package freeze-dried peas
1 package freeze-dried corn
½ cup blanched, slivered almonds
¼ cup dried onion flakes
Water

**At home:** Set aside seasoning packets from rice mixes. Cut instructions from boxes. On each, write "plus 1 cup" to amount of water specified.

Pour each packet of rice into a plastic bag. To each bag of rice add half the chicken, peas, corn, almonds, and onion flakes. Enclose one packet of seasonings and one set of instructions; seal.

**In camp:** Follow instructions from rice package, adding the extra cup of water to reconstitute chicken and other ingredients mixed into rice. The result is a tasty one-pot meal. (No, the almonds do not get soggy. Yes, you should carry the seasonings sealed in their packets; otherwise, they end up clinging to the inside of the plastic bag instead of flavoring your meal.)

## That Good Brown Rice Stuff

**Yield:** One-pot dinner for 4
**Preparation time in camp:** 15 to 20 minutes

*This combination of ingredients blends into a very flavorful and satisfying simple meal.*

1 batch Almost-Instant Brown Rice (the amount of precooked rice
    made by following that recipe)
¾ cup TVP (textured vegetable protein)
½ cup dried onion flakes
½ cup dried tomatoes or tomato flakes
¼ cup dried parsley flakes
2 bouillon cubes (your choice of flavor)
8 cups water

**At home:** Measure all ingredients except water into plastic bag and
seal airtight.

**In camp:** Add 8 cups water, stir together and simmer 15 to 20
minutes, stirring occasionally.

## Goulash

**Serves:** 3
**Preparation time in camp:** 30 minutes

*This is a pack-ahead "mindless meal" that can be prepared easily on a
night when you are disinclined to do anything with food except eat it.
Consider packaging the batch as three separate, one-person dinners.*

3 cups elbow macaroni (plain or assorted vegetable flavors)
1½ cups dried tomatoes
1½ cups TVP (textured vegetable protein), beef flavored
¼ cup dried onion flakes
½ cup dried mushrooms
1 cup tomato sauce, dried into leather and pulverized (see Index)
Water
Salt and cracked black pepper to taste

**At home:** Measure and bag macaroni. Measure and bag together all
other ingredients except water, salt, and pepper.

**In camp:** Bring large pot of unsalted water to a boil. Pour 2 cups of
the water over dry ingredients, cover, and let stand to reconstitute
while cooking macaroni until tender. Drain most of water from
macaroni, reserving it if water is in short supply. Return macaroni to
pot; add vegetables. Stir and simmer, adding water as needed to fully
reconstitute and reach consistency of stew. Add salt and pepper to
taste.

## Old-fashioned Sourdough Pancakes

**Serves:** 2 generously
**Preparation time in camp:** 30 minutes

*Even people who do not usually like pancakes find themselves coming back for second helpings of these light, tender ones.*

1 cup sourdough starter (see Index)
2 eggs (or 5 tablespoons each dried egg powder and water), beaten
2 tablespoons oil
¼ to ½ cup milk (or 1 to 2 tablespoons instant dry milk powder and
     scant ¼ to ½ cup water)
1 teaspoon salt
1 teaspoon baking powder
2 tablespoons sugar

**In camp:** Stir together gently the sourdough starter, eggs, oil, and milk. Sprinkle over surface the salt, baking powder, and sugar; fold in gently. Let batter rest 10 to 15 minutes, then spoon into skillet and bake until golden, turning once.

**Variation:** Gently fold 1 cup fresh berries (of any kind) into batter before cooking. (You can sprinkle berries over the top of pancakes as they bake, but when you flip the pancakes, the berries will fry on the surface of the skillet, making it difficult to clean.)

**Note:** Leftover pancakes? No such thing. Those made from the Old-fashioned Sourdough Pancakes recipe are very good to eat cold later in the day. Think of them as soft flour tortillas or pocket bread to roll up around cheese, refried beans with chopped onion, lunch meat, tuna and sprouts, or peanut butter. Or use them as "mop-ups" with stew, chili, or curry sauce at dinner time.

## Sourdough Pancookies

**Serves:** 1 or more
**Preparation time in camp:** 10 minutes

*When you have had your fill of Old-fashioned Sourdough Pancakes and there is a bit of batter left, stir in a few extra ingredients and bake up a little batch of cookies.*

Leftover pancake batter
Sprinkling of sugar to sweeten to taste
2 pinches cinnamon
1 pinch (each) nutmeg and/or cloves
Raisins
Nuts or sunflower seeds

**In camp:** To pancake batter left in bowl, add the amendments and cook like little pancakes. Cool and pack for a midmorning munch.

## Sourdough Biscuits

**Serves:** 4
**Preparation time in camp:** 1 hour

*These can be baked equally well in a reflector oven, Dutch oven, or bannock-style in a frying pan.*

1 cup sourdough starter (see Index)
2 cups flour (divided)
½ teaspoon salt
1 tablespoon sugar
1 teaspoon baking powder
½ teaspoon baking soda

**In camp:** To sourdough, add about ½ of the first cup of flour and beat well. To flour remaining in cup, add the salt, sugar, baking powder, and soda, mixing well. Add mixture to sourdough and beat again. Gradually stir in second cup of flour to form dough.

Turn the dough out onto floured board and knead, turning, about 10 times. Press into ½-inch thickness and cut into about 12 pieces. Round their corners while placing on baking pan. Cover, shield from draft, and let stand until doubled in size, about 30 to 45 minutes. Bake at medium temperature until golden brown.

## Sourdough Biscuits-on-a-Stick

**Serves:** 4
**Preparation time in camp:** 1 hour

*Not just for youngsters who enjoy toasting their own Biscuits-on-a-Stick, this baking method comes in handy when traveling with a minimum of gear.*

**In camp:** Follow recipe for Sourdough Biscuits (see Index), but pat dough into a thinner sheet (about ¼ inch thick). Cut into 8 rectangles and wrap each one around the peeled end of a stick about the thickness of your thumb. Pinch together edges and end to securely enclose stick. Cover dough and let rise until doubled in bulk (about 30 to 45 minutes). Toast over campfire to bake. When done, biscuit slips easily from stick. Fill biscuit center with butter, honey, or jelly.

# Sourdough Hush Puppies

**Serves:** 4
**Preparation time in camp:** 30 minutes

1 egg (or 2½ tablespoons egg powder and equal amount water)
1 cup sourdough starter (see Index)
¼ cup oil
½ cup milk (or 2 tablespoons instant dry milk powder and scant ½ cup water)
1 cup corn meal
¼ cup sugar
1 teaspoon salt
1 cup flour (divided)
½ teaspoon baking soda
1 tablespoon warm water
Chopped onion (optional)

**In camp:** Break egg into starter and beat egg slightly with tip of spoon. Add oil and milk; blend well. (Beyond this point, fold in ingredients with as little stirring as possible.)

Into center of batter, pour corn meal, sugar, salt, and ½ cup flour. Fold just enough to dampen dry ingredients.

Measure soda into a cup and add warm water. Stir to blend and immediately pour over batter. Add another ½ cup flour (and chopped onion, if desired). Fold to blend.

Drop by tablespoonfuls into hot oil about 1 inch deep. (I use the skillet for this.) Deep-fry until well browned, turning as needed. Drain (on paper towels, if you have any) and serve hot.

# Sourdough Cinnamon Rolls

**Serves:** 4
**Preparation time in camp:** 70 minutes

*Make these for a leisurely brunch. While dough is rising, enjoy juice, coffee, and eggs. Then bring on the warm Sourdough Cinnamon Rolls.*

1 recipe Sourdough Biscuits (see Index)
¼ cup soft margarine
3 to 4 tablespoons sugar
2 teaspoons cinnamon
½ cup raisins (optional)

**In camp:** Follow recipe for Sourdough Biscuits, pressing dough into a rectangle about ½ inch thick. Spread surface with butter, sugar, cinnamon, and raisins. Starting at a long edge of the dough rectangle, roll it up like a jelly roll, enclosing filling. Pinch edge to seal. With a sharp knife, slice roll into ½-inch pieces. Place on pan, cover, and let rise until doubled in bulk (about 30 to 45 minutes). Bake at medium temperature until golden brown. (Wonderful served warm and topped with more margarine or butter.)

# Sourdough Dumplings

**Serves:** 2
**Preparation time in camp:** 30 minutes

*These make a one-pot meal out of any hearty soup or stew. While the soup is simmering, make dumpling batter from:*

½ cup sourdough starter (half the amount used in most recipes)
    (see Index)
1 tablespoon soft margarine or cooking oil
1 cup flour (divided)
Salt to taste
½ teaspoon baking powder
½ teaspoon baking soda

**In camp:** Blend starter with margarine or oil. Stir in ½ the flour. To flour remaining in cup, add salt (as desired), baking powder, and soda, mixing well. Add to sourdough and fold just enough to moisten flour.
    Bring soup or stew to a boil. If stew is thick, add liquid to make it

a pourable consistency. (It needs enough liquid so it will not burn on the bottom while dumplings steam.)

Drop dumpling batter by large spoonfuls onto bubbling soup or stew. Cover and simmer 15 minutes without lifting lid.

# Sourdough Cobbler

**Serves:** 4
**Preparation time in camp:** 30 minutes

*Make this delicious dessert with any combination of fresh-picked berries and/or dried fruits that have been soaked in water to reconstitute.*

½ cup water
½ to 1 cup sugar
1 teaspoon lemon juice
Seasonings: ½ teaspoon (each) cinnamon, cloves, and/or nutmeg, as
    desired, or 2 tablespoons brandy
3 cups fresh berries or reconstituted dried fruits
1 tablespoon sugar
½ cup sourdough starter (half the amount used in most recipes)
    (see Index)
1 cup flour (divided)
½ teaspoon baking powder
½ teaspoon baking soda

**In camp:** In large pot, bring water to boil. Stir in sugar, lemon juice, and seasonings, then berries. Cover and bring to boil. Meanwhile, make batter from remaining ingredients.

Sprinkle sugar over starter. Add ½ the flour and stir to blend well. To flour remaining in cup, add baking powder and soda, mixing thoroughly. Add to sourdough mixture and fold just enough to dampen dry ingredients. Drop by large spoonfuls onto boiling fruit. Cover and simmer 15 minutes. (Do not lift lid, as steam in pot is cooking batter from overhead as hot fruit is cooking it from below.) Serve warm, spooned into bowls.

## Missouri Mix

**Yield:** 12 cups
**Preparation time at home:** 15 minutes
**Preparation time in camp:** Ready to use

*Tom Steinburn, senior guide for Pacific Water Sports, Seattle, is a superb camp cook. Before a trip, he stirs up a batch of multipurpose Missouri Mix to use for biscuits, dumplings, cobbler toppings, and anything else he might take a notion to bake.*

1½ cups shortening
8 cups flour
½ cup baking powder
2 tablespoons salt
1⅓ cups instant dry milk powder
3 cups quick oats

**At home:** Cut together shortening and flour until there are no lumps and mixture has the consistency of meal. Add remaining ingredients and mix thoroughly. Pack in airtight, resealable container.

**In camp:** Just add water (about ¾ cup water to 2 cups Missouri Mix) to make dough for biscuits or dumplings. Add 2 tablespoons sugar to biscuit dough to make cobbler topping. Use Missouri Mix in any recipe that calls for Bisquick or all-purpose baking mix.

## Scones

**Yield:** 6 to 8 wedges
**Preparation time in camp:** 15 minutes

1 tablespoon sugar
1 cup Missouri Mix (see facing page)
1 egg
Scant ¼ cup water
¼ cup raisins or currants

**In camp:** Stir sugar into Missouri Mix. Beat egg into water, add to Missouri Mix, and stir to form soft dough. Add raisins, stirring and kneading to blend. Pat dough into circle ¼ to ½ inch thick. Cut like a pie into wedges. Place slightly apart and bake in greased Dutch oven or bannock-style in skillet (turning frequently) until done. Serve warm with butter and jelly (or bits of fruit leather).

# Tom's Special

**Serves:** 8
**Preparation time in camp:** 20 minutes

*This decadent dessert is a Tom Steinburn improvisation on simple, wholesome Missouri Mix.*

1 batch instant vanilla pudding, made from 3-ounce packaged mix
2 cups Missouri Mix (see Index)
¼ cup sugar
1 teaspoon cinnamon
1 cup water
Brandy or other liquor (optional)

**In camp:** Make vanilla pudding according to package directions. Set aside.

Mix together Missouri Mix, sugar, and cinnamon. Stir in water to make a soft dough. Drop from tablespoon into greased Dutch oven or onto greased baking pan. Bake until done, usually about 12 minutes.

Break warm biscuits into individual bowls. Top with pudding and a splash of brandy, if desired.

# Icy Bay Cinnamon Coffee Cake

**Serves:** 6 to 8
**Preparation time in camp:** 45 minutes

*This recipe from Judy Moyer of Pacific Water Sports, Seattle, is named for Icy Bay in Alaska's Prince William Sound, where the hearty coffee cake was first made in 1979. The baking time given is based on Judy's experience with a ring-type oven that fits atop a campstove.*

1½ cups Bisquick or all-purpose baking mix
½ cup whole wheat flour
½ cup brown sugar
¼ cup instant dry milk powder
1½ teaspoons cinnamon
Dash of nutmeg
Topping: 1 cup (or more) mixed fruits and nuts (raisins, walnuts,
    chopped dates, chopped apple, plus a handful of brown sugar)
1 tablespoon oil
Water

**At home:** In zip locking bag, combine baking mix, flour, sugar, and milk powder. In second zip locking bag, combine cinnamon, nutmeg, and topping.

**In camp:** Pour oil in with baking mix combination. Add water a spoonful at a time, just enough to make a very stiff dough. (Mix by reclosing bag and kneading.) Grease Dutch oven or baking pan; pat dough into it and sprinkle contents of topping bag over surface. Bake 30 minutes or until done.

# Cheesecake

**Serves:** 4
**Preparation time in camp:** 15 minutes to prepare plus 1 hour to stand

*Pack candles in with the cheesecake mix, and you are ready to celebrate a birthday on your kayak trip.*

1 package no-bake cheesecake mix
6 tablespoons instant dry milk powder
2 tablespoons maple syrup
1½ cups water

**At home:** Open cheesecake box and remove both packets of mix (for crust and filling). Put them into plastic bag along with the instructions cut from back of box. Measure milk powder into sandwich bag and close with twist-tie. Enclose in plastic bag and seal.

**In camp:** Into cold skillet, dump contents of crust packet. Drizzle syrup over it. Mix with fingers, then press into skillet, lining skillet with crust. (This is not what the cheesecake package tells you to do but works much better in camp, and tastes better, too.) Set aside.

In small bowl, stir together contents of filling packet and milk powder. Gradually add water, stirring constantly. Beat as best you can. Pour filling into crust and put in a cool place to set for about 1 hour.

Cheesecake is easiest to serve by cutting down through filling and crust with a knife, then lifting each piece with a pancake turner or spatula. A nonstick-finish skillet makes this a piece of cake (if you will pardon the expression). Be careful not to scratch the pan.

**Variation:** When circumstances permit, top with a few fresh-picked berries or a boxful of frozen strawberries (which will keep two days packed in Styrofoam chips).

# Mystery Pudding

**Serves:** 4
**Preparation time in camp:** 10 minutes

3 ounces (1 package) instant vanilla pudding mix
8 tablespoons instant dry milk powder
½ to 1 cup cookie crumbs, broken nuts, pulverized granola, and other
    odds and ends of that ilk
Scant 2 cups cold water
Splash of sherry, rum, or brandy (optional)

**At home:** Mix instant pudding with milk powder and seal in small zip
locking bag. With waterproof marking pen, write the flavor on outside
of bag.

**In camp:** Collect crumbs and other oddments from lunch sacks. Mix
together, crumbling any overly large chunks and rounding out the
collection to make at least ½ cup. Distribute equally in individual bowls
or mugs.
    In wide-mouth poly bottle, combine milk-pudding mixture and
water. Shake vigorously 2 minutes and immediately pour over crumbs,
stirring to combine.
    Distribute spoons and cups of dessert. As diners probe tentatively
at what is in their cups, drizzle sherry or rum over it.

**Variation:** Also try chocolate pudding (with a rounded teaspoonful of
instant coffee stirred into the mix along with the milk powder). It is
best over leftovers that run heavily to chocolate chips and nuts.
Drizzle with rum or brandy.

# Gingerbread

**Serves:** 6 to 8
**Preparation time in camp:** 45 minutes

*This warm gingerbread can be topped with Dream Whip "when you
want to really razzle-dazzle guests," says Judy Moyer, of Pacific Water
Sports, Seattle. Baking time is based on her experience with a ring-type
oven that fits atop a campstove.*

1¾ cups Bisquick or all-purpose baking mix
½ cup brown sugar
1 teaspoon ginger
1 teaspoon cinnamon
½ teaspoon cloves
4 tablespoons dry egg powder
2 tablespoons instant dry milk powder
½ cup water
¼ cup oil
½ cup molasses
Dream Whip topping (optional)

**In camp:** mix together all ingredients except Dream Whip. Grease Dutch oven or baking pan and spread dough in bottom. Bake 30 minutes.

# Swedish Fruit Soup

**Serves:** 4
**Preparation time in camp:** 50 minutes

*A bowl of warm fruit compote for dessert is just the right follow-up to many a one-pot meal.*

½ cup dried apricots
½ cup dried pitted prunes
½ cup dried apple slices
¼ cup currants
¼ cup sugar
2 tablespoons quick tapioca
1 cinnamon stick
3 cups water
2 tablespoons lemon juice
Brandy (optional)

**At home:** Package together all dried fruits. Enclose separate packet containing sugar, tapioca, and cinnamon stick.

**In camp:** Soak fruits in water 30 minutes. Stir in sugar mixture and lemon juice. Bring to boil, reduce heat, cover, and simmer 15 minutes, stirring occasionally. Serve warm, splashed with brandy, if desired.

# Related Reading

## ON CAMP COOKERY

Chambers, Patricia. *River Runners' Recipes*. Seattle: Pacific Search Press, 1984.

Fleming, June. *The Well-Fed Backpacker*. 3d Vintage Books Ed. New York: Random House, Vintage Books, 1986.

McHugh, Gretchen. *The Hungry Hiker's Book of Good Cooking*. New York: Alfred Knopf, 1982.

R.E.I. Co-op. *The Outdoor Epicure*. Seattle: Recreational Equipment Inc., 1979.

## ON FOOD DRYING

MacManiman, Gen. *Dry It – You'll Like It*, enlarged ed. Fall City, Washington: MacManiman Inc., 1980.

Peterson, Una Jean W. *Dehydrating for Food and Fun*. Marysville, Washington: Golden Son Productions, 1976.

## ON FISHING AND FORAGING

*Alaska*® magazine, Editors of. *Alaska Wild Berry Guide and Cookbook*. Edmonds, WA.: Alaska Northwest Publishing Company, 1982.

Challenger, Jean. *How to Cook Your Catch!* 2d (rev.) ed. Sidney, B.C., Canada: Saltaire Publishing Ltd., 1977.

British Columbia Provincial Museum, Handbook series (various titles and authors). Vancouver, B.C., Canada.

Doerper, John. *Shellfish Cookery*. Seattle: Pacific Search Press, 1985.

Graham, Frances Kelso, and the Ouzinkie Botanical Society. *Plant Lore of an Alaskan Island*. Edmonds, WA.: Alaska Northwest Publishing Company, 1985.

White, Charlie. *Living Off the Sea*. Vancouver, B.C., Canada: Maclean Hunter, Special Interest Publications, 1985.

## ON SOURDOUGH

*Alaska®* magazine, Editors of. *Cooking Alaskan*. Anchorage: Alaska Northwest Publishing Company, 1984.

Allman, Ruth. *Alaska Sourdough*. Anchorage: Alaska Northwest Publishing Company, 1976.

## ON NUTRITION

Howe, Phyllis Sullivan. *Basic Nutrition in Health and Disease, Including Selection and Care of Food*, 7th ed. Philadelphia: W.B. Saunders Company, 1981.

Lappé, Frances Moore. *Diet for a Small Planet*, 10th Anniversary Edition. New York: Random House, Ballantine Books, 1982.

Robertson, Laurel; Flinders, Carol; and Godfrey, Bronwen. *Laurel's Kitchen, A Handbook for Vegetarian Cookery and Nutrition*, Bantam Edition. Petaluma, California: Nilgiri Press, 1976; New York: Bantam Books Inc., 1978.

## ON FOOD STORAGE

U.S. Department of Agriculture. Food Safety and Inspection Service. Home and Garden Bulletin No. 241, "The Safe Food Book, Your Kitchen Guide," rev. ed. Washington, D.C.: Government Printing Office, 1984.

Washington State University. College of Agriculture and Home Economics. EB 1205, "Storing Foods at Home." Pullman: Cooperative Extension and the U.S. Department of Agriculture, 1983.

Washington State University, University of Idaho, and Oregon State University. PNW 250, "You Can Prevent Food Poisoning." Pullman: Pacific Northwest Cooperative Extension Bulletins, 1984.

## ON KAYAK TOURING

Dowd, John. *Sea Kayaking, A Manual for Long-Distance Touring,*
   Rev. Ed. Vancouver: Douglas & McIntyre Ltd., 1983.

Washburne, Randel. *The Coastal Kayaker.* Seattle: Pacific Search
   Press, 1983.

# Index